SEXUALLY ABUSED CHILDREN: MAKING THEIR PLACEMENTS WORK

PUBLISHED BY

BRITISH AGENCIES FOR

ADOPTION & FOSTERING

11 SOUTHWARK STREET

LONDON SE1 1RQ

© BAAF 1991

ISBN 0 903534 94 0

DESIGNED BY ANDREW HAIG

TYPESET BY SET TWO CREATIVE TYPESETTING

PRINTED AND BOUND IN ENGLAND

British Agencies for Adoption & Fostering (BAAF) is a registered charity and professional association for all those working in the child care field. BAAF's other publications in this subject area include *Child abuse: the Scottish experience* (edited by Fred Stone, 1989); and *After abuse: caring and planning for a child who has been sexually abused* (by Jenny Robson and Donal Giltinan with Helen Kenward, 1989) available as a three-day training course pack or as a booklet of course papers.

PRACTICE SERIES : 18

Sexually abused children

making their placements work

◆

edited by Daphne Batty

BRITISH AGENCIES FOR
ADOPTION & FOSTERING

Acknowledgements

I have been supported in the editing of this book by Professor Fred Stone, whose constructive criticism has been of great value throughout. The comments of Dr Frank Bamford and Mrs Pat Verity of NFCA have also been very helpful. Without the cheerful co-operation of BAAF secretaries, returning again and again to their word processors, the book would not have reached the printers. My sincere thanks to them all.

Daphne Batty
BAAF

Contents

Foreword

Scarcely a day passes without some reference to the sexual abuse of children, whether in the press, on the radio or on television. Conference follows conference, official enquiries lead to department guidelines, and inevitably publications multiply. How then to justify yet another book on the subject? For a start, there is little evidence that there are any convincing solutions to the problem, nor even that we can confidently trust the facts presented. Certainly it is quite seldom that a rational, balanced viewpoint is expressed. All too evident is the tendency to polarisation – the interests of parents against those who seek to protect their offspring; the social worker and the police confronting each other; the expert witness at odds with the legal process.

One particular aspect of child sexual abuse is of special concern to BAAF, namely the welfare of children in the care of substitute parents. This is the focus of this book. The contributors all have first-hand experience, whether as foster carers, teachers, social workers, psychologists, doctors, or researchers, and with the assistance of Daphne Batty, a supportive but firm editor, have sought to produce a practical manual, emphasising the support required by these children and their families, as well as what is realistically available.

The best antidote to the high drama, scapegoating and fear which the topic seems destined to provoke is the presentation of carefully accumulated findings by experienced workers who are prepared to share their successes and failures with complete honesty.

I commend this publication which seeks to do precisely that.

Fred H Stone, Emeritus Professor of Child and Adolescent Psychiatry, University of Glasgow

January 1991

1 Family attitudes towards children's sexuality

Margaret Grocke

Dr Margaret Grocke is a research psychologist. She was part of a team carrying out research at the Institute for Child Health for the Department of Health regarding understanding of sexuality and sexual thinking in both abused and non-abused children. She here summarises existing research findings in studies of 'normal' families and points to the need for further research in this area.

> (W)e know more about sexual deviance than we do about sexual normality or ordinariness . . . all theories about children's sexual victimisation must be viewed against their true backdrop: a vast ignorance of the forces governing the development and expression of sexual behaviour in general.[1]

Few studies have explored family attitudes towards sexuality. As a result, it is difficult to establish if behaviour patterns in sexually abused children or their families deviate from the norm. Parental attitudes towards behaviour at home such as nudity and physical contact will influence children's sexual concepts, attitudes and behaviour.

The small number of studies that have been undertaken have found a wide variation in family practices, influenced by such factors as the attitudes the parents experienced in their own families as children, their educational level, religious beliefs and other cultural factors. Studies in Western cultures have found a contrast between the philosophies of families from the manual and non-manual social classes. The Newsons, for example, describe this contrast between middle and working class families in their English sample:

> On one end of the scale ' . . . parents subscribe to the view that it is natural, and therefore right and proper, for children to be curious about their bodies, to be interested in the anatomical differences which distinguish the sexes, and to want to know the source of new life. In order to engender "natural", "healthy" attitudes to sex in adult life, they believe that a child's curiosity should be satisfied

frankly and openly, and as early as his [or her] own curiosity dictates.' At the other end, the contrasting philosophy maintains 'that sexual curiosity is suspect, sexual information dangerous and perhaps frightening for the young child and both must be controlled by being suppressed.'[2]

Although the working class families were more repressive in their attitudes towards sexuality, the Newsons suggest that both philosophies argue that a child's 'sexual innocence' should be preserved. While middle class mothers try to neutralise children's curiosity in sex by 'bringing it out in the open' so they can supervise and control interest, the working class mothers tend to suppress any sexual interest by actively discouraging it from the onset. Since the Newsons' research, published in 1968, there may have been some changes in attitudes and behaviour. For example, AIDS and other sexual issues have received more attention in the media and there has been more sex education at school. This may be expected to influence both parental attitudes and children's sexual knowledge.

Masturbation or genital play

Parents often observe their young children 'fondling their genitals'. However, many people prefer not to associate this activity with masturbation, believing children do not masturbate or are not sexually aroused to a point of orgasm before puberty. There is evidence that children deliberately fondle their genitals for pleasure and orgasms have been observed in infants.[3] On occasions genital manipulation may be accompanied by pelvic thrusting movements. Parental reactions to masturbation in children will influence how frequently it happens and in what situations it is observed. Strong taboos and negative attitudes towards masturbation have been maintained through some of the traditional myths (for example, that masturbation is harmful) or through religious philosophies which condemn masturbation.

Gagnon[4] questioned over 1,000 American parents of three- to eleven-year-old children on their attitudes towards masturbation. Although over 80 per cent of parents accepted the fact that most pre-teenage children masturbated, fewer than 65 per cent thought it was all right to do so. In a more recent survey, Goldman and Goldman[5] found that over 85 per cent of Australian undergraduate students accepted masturbation as healthy, although at the same time some students reported initial feelings of guilt and shame.

In Gagnon's survey, fewer than 30 per cent of parents reported having observed their child masturbate. There was a wide variation in parental reports (10 per cent to 53 per cent) and they varied with the age and gender of the child. For example, mothers were more likely to report having observed their son masturbating (46 per cent) than their daughter (28 per cent). Parents of older children were less likely to report that their child had masturbated, perhaps because they had forgotten it had occurred. Also, there would be more opportunity for parents to observe younger children masturbating. An earlier study[6] of pre-pubescent children found that the mothers reported that just over half the boys (56 per cent) had masturbated compared to 30 per cent of girls.

Gagnon found that parents who reported a higher incidence of masturbation were more likely to have a higher level of education and more liberal sexual attitudes.[7] Church attenders were more likely to have less positive views and report less behaviour than non-church attenders. The survey also found that parents who said they masturbated themselves were more likely to report that their children masturbated. The Newsons found a social class difference in their families: more mothers from the unskilled working class group punished genital play in their four-year-old children while only five per cent of mothers in the professional and managerial groups reported doing this.

Children's sexual knowledge

Children's curiosity about their bodies also extends to questions about 'where babies come from'. Most four- or five-year-old children know some general facts about how babies grow 'inside mummy's tummy', but few have any knowledge of intercourse.[8] These younger children see the role of the father as being mainly concerned with caring for the mother. By the time children are nine to 11 years of age, most have a general idea about how babies are made, and children over the age of nine are aware that not all women have babies.[9] Studies suggest that there is a developmental progression in children's concepts about reproduction and that their understanding is related to their cognitive development rather than to any developmental maturation.[10] There are a large number of other factors which may influence children's knowledge and understanding, for example the family size, whether there are opposite-sex siblings in the family, the family's educational level and general cultural influences and child-rearing practices.[11]

Most studies have found that mothers are the main source of information on sexual matters at home. Sexual topics still remain taboo in our society and many children do not ever discuss sexual matters with their parents. Allen[12] found that over 40 per cent of teenagers had not spoken to their parents about sex. She also found that girls are more likely to talk to their mothers about sexual matters than boys. Farrell[13] found that middle class children are more likely to learn about reproduction at an earlier age than working class children and that working class children were less likely to be first told about reproduction by their parents.

The peer group is also an important source of information for teenagers. However, information from peers may often be based on half truths or misconceptions. As children get older, school becomes the most important source of their information, as most children receive some sex education at school.

Sexual curiosity and sexual play
It is widely acknowledged that children play sexual games, but it is not clear how common they are or of what type. Sexual play among children may include 'looking' at another child's genitals ('you show me yours and I'll show you mine') or mutual undressing. In some cases, genital contact may occur or vaginal or anal orifices may be penetrated (for example, 'doctor games' may be used as an excuse to examine an opposite-sex child's sex organs or insert an object into an orifice). Sexual play amongst children usually involves mutual exploration. It will usually happen between the child and a friend or sibling without the knowledge of parents. Most children do not talk to their parents about these activities, mainly because of their feared negative reactions from parents or adults. They are likely to decrease as children get older and become more modest, before adolescent sexual activities begin.

Several retrospective studies of undergraduate students suggest that this sort of sexual play is a relatively common occurrence. Haugaard and Tilly,[14] for example, in a retrospective study of 1,000 undergraduates by anonymous questionnaires, found that 42 per cent of students reported having had sexual encounters with another child. Half of these encounters involved sexual hugging and kissing and one or both children exposing themselves or looking at genitals. Nearly half were single encounters and most involved friends. Those who reported that they felt a high level of coercion from the other child rated the experience as more negative than those who did not feel coerced. The sexual act itself was not associated with the person's positive or negative reaction.

Another study, by Goldman and Goldman,[15] surveyed 1,000 first-year Australian undergraduate students, 82 per cent of whom reported some kind of sexual experience with another person before the age of 12 years. Sixty per cent of these encounters were with another child. Fifteen per cent of the students, mostly females, said that they felt negative about the experiences. The majority of them (63 per cent) had told no one about these experiences and most of them said that they did not feel the need to tell anyone at the time. Not surprisingly, given adult attitudes towards these activities, only six per cent told their mothers and two per cent their fathers.

Family patterns of behaviour
One of the few comprehensive studies examining family attitudes and behaviours has been conducted in the USA by Rosenfeld and colleagues. [16, 17, 18, 19] They surveyed 576 upper-middle class families with children from two to ten years by postal questionnaire. The questions asked for information about how 'typical' families rear their children in relation to children's modesty, bath practices, genital touching and sleeping patterns. They were also interested to find out if the pattern of behaviour had changed (and if so, how, why and when).

Bathing patterns
In Rosenfeld's survey, age was the main factor which determined if children bathed alone or with others.[20] Older children bathed less often with their siblings than younger children. Children need less help with bathing as they grow older and only 13 per cent of parents of ten-year-old children said that they needed any help. Mothers reported that they bathed with their daughters more frequently than fathers did with sons. However, it was uncommon for children to bathe with their parents over the age of eight or nine years. Some parents change

11

bathing patterns because a child becomes sexually curious, for example playing sexual games with a sibling or asking questions about a parent's genitals. Of the families in Rosenfeld's survey a large number of families (43 per cent) gave no reason for changes in bathing practices; 12 per cent said that the rule was made by a parent; 19 per cent said that the children had become more modest and they themselves or a sibling had asked to bathe alone; 23 per cent said that the change was made for convenience and two per cent specified other reasons.

Genital touching

It is not uncommon for younger children to touch their parents' genitals, either due to the children's natural urge to explore and touch or to their sexual curiosity. The frequency of touching will be directly related to the opportunities the child has (for example, if the parent is nude or if the child takes baths with the parent) and to the parent's positive or negative reaction to the touching. This exploratory behaviour tends to decrease as children get older.

Rosenfeld's survey[21] suggests that more children touch their mother's genitalia (breasts and/or genitals) than their father's genitals, and daughters touch their mother's genitalia more than sons. Thirty per cent of parents reported that their daughter never touched her father's genitals (at all ages to ten years). In contrast, 45 per cent of parents of eight- to ten-year-old boys reported that they had touched their mother's breasts and/or genitals at some stage. It was not clear what part of the genital area the child touched (pubic hair, penis or scrotum). Breasts were not differentiated from genitalia. Children would be more likely to touch their mother's breasts than their genitals, especially if they had been breastfed.

Rosenfeld notes that they were unable to differentiate the type of touching from the parents' comments on the postal questionnaires and suggests it is important to be able to differentiate between touching when a person is nude and in close physical contact with a child and more intentional, exploratory touching.

Nudity

The Newsons[22] found that middle class families were more liberal in their attitudes towards children seeing parents naked than the working class groups. While nearly 60 per cent of four-year-old children from social classes I and II saw both their parents naked, this happened in less than a quarter of families in social classes IV and V.

A similar class difference was found in American families in another study in the 1960s reported by Elias and Gebhard.[23] Nudity was more frequent for both girls and boys in upper-white-collar workers' homes (over 40 per cent) in comparison to blue-collar workers' homes (less than three per cent). The pattern of nudity in families seems to reflect the differences in underlying attitudes towards sexuality between the social classes.

Sleeping patterns

Children commonly come into their parents' bed during the night if they wake up ill or frightened. Rosenfeld found that half of the children aged eight to ten years still came into the parents' bed on occasions, but less than one per cent spent the night there.[24] The behaviour of the middle class families in his study matched recommendations from a number of prominent child-rearing 'experts' (for example, Dr Spock) who have recommended that it is not wise for a child to sleep in the parental bed all night.

There are distinct cultural norms which influence family sleeping patterns. Japanese children, for example, will always sleep in a room with someone else, even if an empty room is available. In contrast, the American attitude is that it is best for children to have a room of their own as soon as possible. This reflects the high value placed on privacy within American culture.

Current research

Most of the studies cited have been conducted in the USA and were often restricted to a middle class sample. A current study (Smith and Grocke[25]), based in the Department of Child Psychiatry at the Institute of Child Health, investigated 150 families and explored parental attitudes and behaviour and children's sexual knowledge in a stratified, random sample of families from the London area. The primary caretaker, usually the mother, and one child aged between four and 16 years in each family were interviewed separately at home. Initial results show a similar pattern to previous studies indicating differences between the social class groups in attitudes and philosophies towards child rearing. More detailed results from this survey will be published.

Summary

Children are often curious about sexual matters and retrospective reports suggest that sexual play amongst young children is relatively common. However, most of these activities occur without their parents' knowledge. Children's sexual knowledge will be derived from a number of different sources, including their peers, parents (mainly their mothers) and school.

Parental attitudes towards sexuality, religious beliefs, social class and other factors will influence both the patterns of behaviour observed in the family and the parent's report of the occurrence of sexual behaviour. Changes in family behaviour over time may reflect children's cognitive and physical development. For example, as children get older, they develop a sense of privacy and many children request to take baths alone and become self-conscious about nudity.

Clearly, behaviour such as children taking baths with parents or touching their parent's genitalia are not uncommon occurrences in families with younger children. This suggests that the behaviour by itself is not abusive, but that the context within which it occurs must be closely examined before any conclusions regarding abuse are reached.

There is a need for more information on normative behaviour in 'typical' families. In future research, it would be interesting to examine how fathers' attitudes towards sexuality and child rearing differ from those of mothers and how this influences the pattern of family behaviour. In addition, we need to identify mechanisms that influence the development and continuation of family attitudes and philosophies towards sexuality as well as the contribution of different cultural and religious factors. The behaviour reported in 'normal' families needs to be contrasted with the patterns observed in families where abuse has occurred. Differences identified may help professionals to evaluate abusive behaviour more accurately and to identify children who are at risk.

References

1 Finkelhor D *Sexually victimized children* Collier Macmillan, 1979.

2 Newson J and Newson E *Four years old in an urban community* George Allen and Unwin, 1968.

3   Bakwin H 'Erotic feelings in infants and young children' *American journal of diseases in childhood* 126, 1973.

4   Gagnon J 'Attitudes and responses of parents to pre-adolescent masturbation' *Archives of sexual behaviour* 14 5, 1985.

5   Goldman R and Goldman J *Show me yours. What children think about sex* Penguin, 1988.

6   Elias J and Gebhard P 'Sexuality and sexual learning in childhood' *Phi delta kappan* 50 7, 1969.

7   See 4 above.

8   Cohen B and Parker S 'Sex information among nursery-school children' in Oremland E and Oremland J (eds) *The sexual and gender development of young children: the role of the educator* Cambridge Massachusetts: Ballinger, 1987.

9   Goldman R and Goldman J *Children's sexual thinking. A comparative study of children aged 5 to 15 years in Australia, North America, Britain and Sweden* Routledge & Kegan Paul, 1982.

10 Bernstein A and Cowan P 'Children's concepts of how people get babies' *Child development* 46 1, 1975. See also 9 above.

11 See 9 above.

12 Allen I *Education in sex and personal relationships* Policy Studies Institute (Research Report No 665) Frances Pinter, 1987.

13 Farrell C and Kellaher L *My mother said . . . The way young people learned about sex and birth control* Routledge & Kegan Paul, 1978.

14 Haugaard J and Tilly C 'Characteristics predicting children's responses to sexual encounters with other children' *Child abuse and neglect* 12, 1988.

15 See 5 above.

16 Rosenfeld A, O'Reilly Wenegrat A, Haavik D, Wenegrat B and Smith C, 'Sleeping patterns in upper middle class families when the child awakens ill or frightened' *Archives of general psychiatry* 39, 1982.

17 Rosenfeld A, Seigel-Gorelick B, Haavik D, Duryea M, Wenegrat A, Martin J and Bailey R 'Parental perceptions of children's modesty: a cross-sectional survey of ages 2-10 years' *Psychiatry* 47, 1984.

18 Rosenfeld A, Bailey R, Siegel B and Bailey G 'Determining incestuous contact between parent and child: frequency of children touching parents' genitals in a nonclinical population' *Journal of the American academy of child psychiatry* 25 4, 1986.

19 Rosenfeld A, Siegel B and Bailey R 'Familial bathing patterns: im-
    plications for cases of alleged molestation and for pediatric practice'
    Pediatrics 79 2, 1987.

20 See 19 above.

21 See 18 above.

22 See 2 above.

23 See 6 above.

24 See 16 above.

25 Smith M and Grocke M *Self-concepts and cognitions about sexuality in
    abused and non-abused children: An experimental study* Report to the
    Department of Health, unpublished.

2 The abused child in the substitute family: the family's perspective

Catherine Macaskill

Catherine Macaskill, who is well known as a researcher in the field of adoption and fostering, considers in this chapter some issues arising from her 1989 research project covering 80 placements of abused children. She looks in particular at the importance to the carers of full information about the child, and at the impact both on the adults and on other children in the families. She draws throughout on the carers' own words. A full report on the project will be published by Batsford in 1991 under the title *Adopting or fostering a sexually abused child.*

During 1989 I was awarded the 'Which?' Jubilee Award by The Consumers' Association to undertake a study of the day-to-day experiences of families caring for sexually abused children. This paper draws exclusively on the material obtained through this study, which comprised interviews with 66 substitute families in Britain. Some were undertaking short-term fostering, others long-term fostering or adoption. All the placements referred to occurred between 1985 and 1989.

The background
The 66 families who took part in the study were nominated by the social services department or voluntary agency responsible for their placements. Most adoptive families had only cared for one sexually abused child. Other families were highly experienced, not only with 'hard-to-place' children, but had also fostered as many as ten to 12 sexually abused children. The 66 families comprised 55 couples and 11 single parents. All were interviewed in the relaxed atmosphere of their own home. In order to keep the focus of each interview as clear as possible, each family was asked to discuss only one placement. Some chose the most difficult placement they had tackled; others preferred to concentrate on the most rewarding one; while several wanted to use the interview to talk about a placement which had disrupted. Exceptions to the rule of discussing one placement only were sibling placements. In this way a total of 80 placements – 50

girls and 30 boys – were studied in detail, with ages at placement ranging from three months to 18 years. Varying lengths of placements were represented, ranging from three months to seven years.

Defining sexual abuse

At the outset of the study the term 'sexual abuse' was not defined. Faced with general information about the broad aims of the study, statutory and voluntary agencies themselves decided which families should be included and excluded, using their own criteria to define sexual abuse. As a result the families nominated had often handled placements where abuse was an unmistakable and significant feature.

In the context of this study it was rare for children to be mere observers of sexual activity. The norm was for them to be intimately involved in some type of sexual act, ranging from touching and fondling through to full sexual intercourse. Anal, oral or vaginal abuse were sometimes also associated with cruelty. Physical objects such as knitting needles, toothbrushes, knives and sticks were all used in children's genitals. Torture featured in some cases. Restraining children, tying them to beds, and gagging, shaving and burning pubic hair were additional distressing aspects. Sex rings occurred, with a complex network of grandparents, uncles, aunts, cousins and their associates participating in sexual rituals with all age groups of children. Young children's bodies were sold for financial rewards. Children as young as seven or eight were themselves forced to attempt sexual intercourse while the act was videoed and later sold as pornography.

Of course, every aspect of sexual abuse was not necessarily associated with pain and cruelty. The fact that there were enjoyable aspects in some cases merely exacerbated the problem, adding confusion and tension to the child's internal turmoil.

Additional factors in children's background histories

Sexual abuse was only one factor in the child's history and it must be viewed within the context of a multiplicity of problems. Many children lived in impoverished family environments with the quality of parental care only too frequently being called into question. A number of children were on 'At risk' registers due to injuries such as bruising, burning, inexplicable fractures or in some cases just general

18

professional dissatisfaction with the level of physical and emotional care. Sometimes concern about another sibling was the trigger which sparked off care proceedings for the entire family. Alcoholism, drug addiction and mental illness were factors appearing and reappearing on case records. In situations where one parent had turned to prostitution, children frequently witnessed or were part of the harrassment or physical cruelty associated with this lifestyle. Murder of another child or adult occurred in more than one case and was sometimes the crisis which led to admission into care. Children were not shielded from the darker aspect of life when a parent made a serious suicide attempt. In one case, for instance, an eight-year-old boy actually watched his father commit suicide.

For many children reception in and out of care had become a way of life. Fifty-eight of the 80 children had previous experience of either being in residential care or some type of family placement. Twenty-six had experienced disruption of an adoption or fostering placement at an earlier stage and some children had lived through a series of disruptions.

Figure 1 illustrates that in every case the abuser was a member of the immediate family or the extended family or was already known to the family or child. Abuse by father was the most common. Sometimes the father was the active abuser but the mother would physically restrain the child to enable the abuse to occur. The mother was the sole or predominant abuser in only two cases.

There were eight cases of abuse occurring within foster or adoptive families. Sometimes fostering abuse did not come to light until after an adoption placement had occurred. Professionals who had been responsible for the original placement were often aghast and liable to accuse the new family of a misguided diagnosis.

Very few cases were substantiated in court. In only 15 out of 80 cases was there any type of criminal conviction. In one case as many as nine people were imprisoned. Cases were frequently dropped because there was insufficient evidence, and sometimes children retracted their story. When the child's disclosure occurred after being placed for adoption the adoptive family were often reluctant to instigate criminal proceedings in case it would create a degree of distress which would impede the progress of the placement.

19

Figure 1. **Who is the perpetrator or alleged perpetrator?**
Number of cases of child sexual abuse

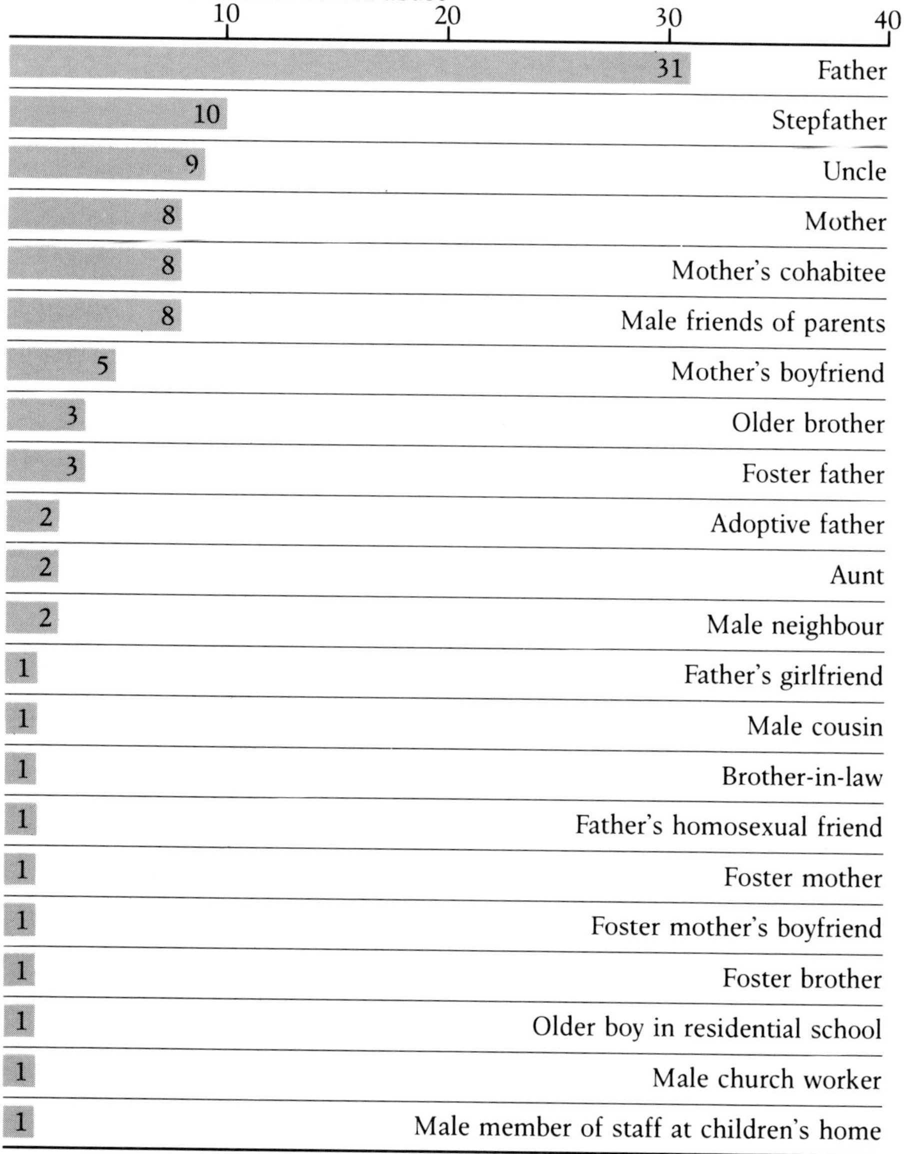

Number of cases	Perpetrator
31	Father
10	Stepfather
9	Uncle
8	Mother
8	Mother's cohabitee
8	Male friends of parents
5	Mother's boyfriend
3	Older brother
3	Foster father
2	Adoptive father
2	Aunt
2	Male neighbour
1	Father's girlfriend
1	Male cousin
1	Brother-in-law
1	Father's homosexual friend
1	Foster mother
1	Foster mother's boyfriend
1	Foster brother
1	Older boy in residential school
1	Male church worker
1	Male member of staff at children's home

Total number of perpetrators: 101

In many cases abuse was being perpetrated by more than one adult.

SEXUAL ABUSE: AN UNKNOWN FACTOR

In 34 per cent of the cases, families had no knowledge of sexual abuse being an issue at the point when the placement occurred.

Figure 2 **Substitute families' knowledge of sexual abuse before or after placement**

	Number	Per cent
Definite knowledge of abuse *before* placement	40	50%
Suspected abuse *before* placement	13	16%
Knowledge of abuse emerged *after* placement (not considered before)	27	34%
Total	80	100%

Given that all the placements occurred between 1985 and 1989, it is alarming to discover that the fact that the child had been sexually abused was sometimes concealed from the substitute family even when the professionals involved knew about it. This happened in six placements. Social workers did not always consider it relevant to mention sexual abuse, even when it was a key factor surrounding the child's reception into care.

> The feeling they gave us was that they were not telling for our benefit. It wouldn't be good for us to know.

Other families conceded that the information was omitted through professional thoughtlessness rather than by deliberate design. In two cases foster carers were shocked to discover information about sexual abuse for the first time through a casual remark made by a social worker at a major case conference. One adoptive father was adamant about the reasons for hiding the information from his family:

> They're selling the child to us. They don't want to release the bad facts. Sexual abuse is not a good selling point.

On whatever basis the professional decision to withhold such key information was made, it often had dramatic consequences for families, as the following story illustrates.

21

> Social services placed an eleven-year-old boy with me. No one told
> me anything about sexual abuse (I found out afterwards that they
> did know the full history of this case). The social worker said that
> he was a confused child who didn't know male from female
> (whatever does that mean, I thought!) and that he needed lots of
> love and affection. So I gave him lots of cuddles. This child used to
> throw himself from one side of the room to the other. He would
> come up to me and touch my leg. I used to get the most awful vibes
> from that (but I kept thinking, The social worker says 'Give him
> love and affection'). Then one day he turned and looked into my
> eyes and said, 'I like you mum'. I responded, 'I like you too'. Then
> the bombshell came: 'When am I going to have sex with you?' All
> the other children were lying on the floor watching TV. They all
> turned round and stared . . . I was speechless.

Of course it was not always the case that professionals withheld
significant information about sexual abuse. In 21 cases they themselves were completely unaware of the sexual abuse diagnosis at the
point of placement. Frequently this aspect only emerged as children
began to feel secure enough to divulge sensitive details of their past
history to members of the substitute family. As a result some families,
who had at an earlier stage categorically stated that they did not want
to take on a sexually abused child, described themselves as 'thrown in
at the deep end'. Naturally, they felt cheated:

> It was a bit like saying to the hospital 'Whatever happens, do not
> take my leg off'. You waken up suddenly and you think 'Gosh,
> help! my leg has been amputated . . .' It was exactly the opposite of
> what we had asked for.

One foster family took on Mark (three-and-a-half years) as their
first foster child. His history included details of physical abuse. On
more than one occasion hospital admission had been essential due
to cigarette marks and bruises appearing on his body. As Mark
began to settle, his foster carers became aware of a series of behaviour
signs which they interpreted as 'unusual'. The idea that these signs
might have some connection with sexual abuse did not cross their
minds:

> There were certain things about Mark that we could not put our
> finger on. Whenever one of us put him on the pot he would look

over his shoulder very warily. My husband used to take him on his knee and play Humpty Dumpty. He was terrified. Any kind of rough and tumble game made him hysterical. If my husband tried to wash his hair or bath him he got very distressed . . . he had problems sleeping. He would take three or four hours to sleep. He would lie staring at the ceiling with a vacant expression on his face. Once you put him to bed he would never get up. He seemed rooted to the spot.

Five months into the placement this family was dumbfounded when Mark suddenly announced one evening:

Daddy used to bite my willy winkle and I used to bite his too.

Three hours later Mark was still talking. Once he had uttered his first sentence, it was as if a valve had been released and the entire story began to pour out.

Failure to recognise the importance of early warning signs of abuse was a particular feature of the placement of boys. Many families acknowledged that they had tended to associate sexual abuse solely with teenage girls. One single parent on first hearing about her twelve-year-old boy's sexual abuse found it difficult to conceal her dismay:

I was puzzled. My first thought was 'How is it possible? How can people sexually abuse a boy?'

In another placement a very experienced foster mother had herself been sexually abused. This fact remained a secret which she had never shared with her husband, nor with anyone else. She had fostered a wide range of 'hard-to-place' children. Privately she had felt that she would never want to foster a sexually abused child, but she had never verbalised this thought to anyone. When four-year-old Steven was placed with her no one suspected that sexual abuse had occurred. One evening, when she was bathing Steven, he began his story with the following sentence:

Grandad used to hurt my ding dong.

These words not only had major implications for this child, they also presented this foster mother with a personal crisis. Could she continue to conceal her own abuse while simultaneously helping this child? Major decisions had to be made quickly. One alternative was to bring the placement to an abrupt end. The other was for her to expose a painful secret which had been gnawing inside her for years.

> The whole sexual abuse thing made me feel quite ill. A foster friend said to me, 'Don't look after him any more' . . . but he had had such a raw deal already.

> I was frightened. I had been abused myself. That made it worse. That was really why I had such a 'thing' about it.

> I will always be grateful to Steven – more grateful than he can ever know. Through him I began to talk about my own abuse for the first time. It gave me an opportunity to open up to my husband about it. In some ways this placement was the best thing that ever happened.

Her comments, and the other examples in this section, should alert social workers to the necessity of preparing all substitute families for the possibility that they may unexpectedly find themselves parenting a sexually abused child. It is impossible to guarantee to any family that a sexually abused child will not be placed with them.

The relevance of full background information
Even when families were told that the child had been sexually abused, many complained that the information which they received was too scant.

> They've told us she's been sexually abused. They think that's sufficient. They haven't given us any details or any guidance.

Another family, who made the following comment, felt seriously disadvantaged:

> They never told us WHO abused, WHEN abuse occurred, WHAT type of abuse, WHERE abuse happened.

Some families were unsure about whether they had the right to request additional information on such an intimate subject. They feared that their questions might be interpreted as 'prying'.
    One difficult fostering placement of a 14-year-old, Sally, disrupted following a crisis which probably could have been averted if the foster

family had received more detailed information. The sudden termination of this placement occurred one evening when Sally decided that she wanted to go to bed early and the foster mother was filling a hot water bottle for her. While they were standing together in the kitchen, Sally suddenly snatched the bottle out of the foster mother's hands and threw the boiling water in her face. Several weeks later, the foster mother obtained access to more detailed case material about Sally. Imagine her dismay when she discovered for the first time that a hot water bottle had been part of Sally's original experience of sexual abuse. The social worker had not had the foresight to share this information with the foster carers. While it is clear that such specific information may not be readily available in every case, this example should alert social workers to the need to obtain the most comprehensive data in every case and to recognise that seemingly minor pieces of information concerning a child's sexual abuse may have profound implications for day-to-day living.

In another example a teenager had developed a pattern of appearing downstairs every morning around seven o'clock and behaving in a very sexualised manner towards the foster father. Initially he did not grasp the significance of the time of day because the family had not been informed that abuse by this girl's stepfather had usually occurred between 7 am and 8 am, immediately after his return home from night shift. As soon as the foster family received this information they became more sensitive to the girl's vulnerability at the beginning of each day and they devised strategies to help her manage this difficult time.

Sometimes an absence of partnership between different professionals was the central reason why the substitute family failed to receive significant background information. One of the worst examples of this concerned a ten-year-old boy placed for adoption on the basis of 'suspicion of abuse'. Eighteen months later, when the placement was in a state of collapse, the adoptive family were startled to discover that the boy had actually disclosed details of his abuse during a therapy session about two years prior to the placement. This information had never been passed on by the psychotherapist to the fostering and adoption department because the therapist perceived it as 'confidential'. Consequently, when the child was placed for adoption this crucial factor was completely omitted from his background details. This placement eventually disrupted. Lack of information was one of a number of factors which the adopters felt had militated against the success of the placement. In the case of each individual child to be placed, social workers should be prepared to raise, with all the professionals involved, the issue of confidentiality vis-à-vis openness and their possible significance for placement outcome.

The sexual element: its impact on the substitute family

The impact on adults in the family
Children's histories of sexual abuse evoked strong reactions in some foster and adoptive families. In rare cases cuddling, holding or comforting the child became problematic because of the revulsion felt towards the abuser and towards the fact that the child's body had been violated. A few reported that the child's flesh was 'creepy' or even 'repugnant'. These emotions had to be overcome if the placement was to succeed.

Even the physical space which the child occupied in the family could take on negative connotations. One foster mother acknowledged how uncomfortable she felt when she approached the abused teenager's bedroom:

> She moved into a bedroom which had been occupied by my ten-year-old son. It had been a very nice homely room . . . She used to write obscene words on the wall. I used to hate going into it. It had such a powerful, hateful, hostile feeling. It made me feel that I was not welcome there.

Few families engaged in this work without having to handle some type of sexualised behaviour from the abused child. In some cases this behaviour was directed solely towards adults while in others it was children who were the main targets for sexual advances. It is important to point out, however, that sexualised behaviour was not an automatic outcome in every case. In as small a proportion of placements as 16 out of 80 (20 per cent) there were no overt sexual approaches towards either adults or children.

When they did occur, overtures such as sexual touching or demands for sexual intercourse seemed to be reserved for one parent in the foster or adoptive family. There did not seem to be any definite pattern about which parent was approached. For example, it did not automatically follow that children would act sexually towards the parent of the same sex as their abuser. One highly experienced parent, commenting on sexual episodes with a ten-year-old foster boy, suggested that the gender of the parent was immaterial:

> He was sitting opposite me flirting with me. I don't think that it would have mattered too much if I had been the dog or the cat. He had been sexually abused by his father, who was the main carer. Okay, I was female – but I was still the main carer.

It was not unusual for the parent who was receiving sexual overtures to experience rejection simultaneously from the child. The form which rejection took varied from case to case. It could be a blanket refusal to communicate, a fretful withdrawal, or a more aggressive approach which included physical onslaughts of abuse. The fact that this parent often had no rapport with the child other than this attempted sexual rapport made it exceptionally difficult for the family to know exactly how to respond.

Even very young children were capable of sexualised behaviour. Patricia was only three years old, but her behaviour had clear sexual overtones.

> Patricia was so disturbed at night. She would waken in the middle of the night to masturbate. She would lie on the bed with her legs wide apart. It was an obvious invitation to me to 'come on'.

Adoptive or foster fathers only occasionally provided useful insights into how difficult the experience of sexual touching had been for them. Perhaps because more interviews were completed with women than with men, this featured more frequently with foster and adoptive mothers. A number of women felt strongly that it was an issue which literature on sexual abuse had failed to address. Families who had participated in training courses felt that it was a glaring omission from these programmes also.

> Courses talk about men protecting themselves. Why do they never talk about the mum? It was the most creepy thing that I ever experienced. Nobody prepared me for that.

The sentiments expressed by one adoptive mother were echoed in other interviews also.

He touched the top of my breast. My blood ran cold. I could feel the imprint of his hand for hours afterwards. I felt like I was being abused.

Adults were not indifferent to children's sexual overtures. At least one adoptive father acknowledged during the course of the interview that touching had the effect of making him feel sexually aroused. Another single adoptive mother surprised herself by her reaction.

I used to be puzzled about how a mother could sexually abuse her son. But the whole thing has created problems in me. A lot of what he has been saying and doing has stirred me up. I had not expected that. It has awakened my own sexual needs as a female. It is something that I have not really resolved – and it took me completely by surprise.

Children who had been treated as sexual partners in their own home environment expected an identical pattern when they joined their foster or adoptive family.

Shortly after they came, our own girls went to grandma's for the weekend. Our foster girls Amy (seven) and Emma (four) went frantic. I could not get them to go to bed. In the end it turned out that they assumed that my husband usually went to bed with our girls and as they were away they thought, 'It'll be us tonight'.

Some children had developed the technique of using their bodies sexually to gain favour with their abuser. Now, replicating these patterns of behaviour with their foster and adoptive families, they were confused to discover that they were unable to achieve the same results:

One of the girls had a horrific tantrum. She was threatening to throw herself out of the window. She stormed upstairs shouting a load of abuse. At 6 pm she appeared on the stairway in the most revealing nightie. She started crawling downstairs face forward on her stomach. She had her face up towards me. Everything about her was provocative. She put her hands on my legs and started to sidle up my legs. It was her way of saying 'sorry'. It was learned behaviour.

There was immense confusion in some children's minds about the roles of individuals in the family. The case of 12-year-old Tim vividly portrays this. Tim's father died when he was seven years old. Since his father's death his mother had used him as her regular sexual partner. Consequently, sexual activity between mother and son had become the norm for Tim. A high degree of patience and understanding was essential as Tim brought his own skewed interpretation of relationships into his new family:

> He asks me, if I love him why can I not show it in a physical way? He wants sex. To him that's what mums and sons do. He needs cuddling. The problem is how to allow him the contact he needs and where to draw the line.

> When he approaches me suggestively, I reject him. I used to say to him 'You're approaching me as a boyfriend.' He had no idea what I meant and he used to get so frustrated.

Some children had been involved in a three-way sexual relationship with their parents. This frequently involved the child being taken into bed with both parents when sexual intercourse occurred, and being invited or forced to participate in the sexual act. Twelve-year-old Susan had experienced this type of family lifestyle. When she was placed for adoption with Jane and Ray Smith she made valiant efforts to instigate the same type of sexual behaviour with her new family. Whenever any physical contact occurred between Jane and Ray, Susan quickly imitated this behaviour. For example, when Jane sat on Ray's knee, Susan would jump on as soon as Jane got off and want to receive the same warm caresses from Ray. The Smith family found this very difficult to manage. Privately Jane seethed with anger, but she did not find it easy to admit to anyone just how jealous she felt. On the other hand Ray felt sorry for Susan because she had missed out on so much physical attention. Denying Susan this type of warm physical contact was, in his mind, equated with failing to meet one of the child's most basic needs. In some placements these situations ignited all sorts of unexpected emotional responses and could all too easily escalate to crisis.

Susan's case is just one example of how adept children are at creating rifts between adults. Many more examples could be cited. In one placement where the parents separated and the placement disrupted, the adoptive father did not conceal the fact that the stresses of the placement had contributed to divorce proceedings. In other placements families readily acknowledged how divisive the child's behaviour had been:

> She tried to drive a wedge between us. She used me as a weapon with my husband. She would skirt around him looking for a reaction. He found it difficult. She thought that she was an adult. She was trying to compete for a higher place in the family than a child's.

The impact on other children in the family

Eighty-six per cent of the placements were made with families who already had other children, ranging in age from young babies to adolescents. There was no definite pattern associated with the place occupied by the sexually abused child in the family. Twenty-three children were placed as the youngest family member and eight as the oldest. Some families were large, comprising foster, adoptive and step-children. A few families had one or more children with disabilities. Occasionally a sexually abused child was very close in age to another child in the family. Some foster families cared for several sexually abused children simultaneously.

Most families made some attempt to prepare the other children in a general way for the arrival of a new foster or adoptive child. Very few made any effort in advance of the placement to talk with their children about the sexual abuse aspect and how this might affect them. Some felt that this would be unfair on the new child, while others were concerned about instigating prejudice or fear. At times it seemed premature to talk about facts which might later be disproved. The most common approach was for parents to make general comments to their children like:

> If X does anything unusual let us know immediately.

With this word of caution underpinning the placement, parents approached the task with their eyes and ears open. They were ready to intervene if anything of an inappropriate sexual nature began to affect the other children.

There was clear evidence that bringing a sexually abused child into the family placed the other children in a vulnerable situation, especially when they were not adequately forewarned about potential difficulties. With hindsight some families felt that they had made a mistake by not talking with their own children from the outset. One family who fostered a 12-year-old girl made a conscious decision not to talk with their teenage boys about the sexual abuse aspect of the case. Privately they reasoned:

A twelve-year-old girl would never want to confide in adolescent boys on such an intimate subject.

Within days of the placement they were proved completely wrong. They learned by hard experience that this is an area of work where assumptions can easily be misguided. The family resolved that they would include their boys more fully in all future placements.

However attuned parents were to their own children's needs, sexually abused children often exerted an influence before parents had time to intervene. Occasionally abused children decided to tell their story to a child in the family rather than to an adult. There were instances of children as young as two-and-a-half being involved in this way. In another case a four-year-old boy disclosed unexpectedly to his foster family late one evening after all the other children had gone to bed. The next morning, as soon as he was awake, he rushed into the eight-year-old girl's bedroom and, while she was getting ready for school, he poured out his entire story to her. Naturally, she was startled. She had never heard anyone talk about this type of thing before. Her parents were themselves still recovering from the shock of the disclosure which had occurred less than 24 hours previously. They had not had adequate time to do the groundwork with her.

Sometimes one of the children in the family happened to be present when a disclosure was made to an adult. This happened to ten-year-old Kerry who suffered from cerebral palsy. By chance she was in the bedroom with her mother when her four-year-old adoptive brother Karl started to talk about his abuse for the first time. Karl expressed anger, bitterness and resentment. With his adoptive mother pinned to the wall, he began hitting and biting her as his disjointed story slowly emerged. Looking on, Kerry feared that her mother would be injured. She could not understand the complex dynamics of this emotional scene. In this situation Kerry's mother not only had to cope with Karl's distress but also had to produce simple explanations to pacify her daughter.

Sexually abused children brought an increased awareness of sexual issues into the family. Some families talked about their children's 'innocence being destroyed' as they listened to lurid stories of abuse.

31

SEXUALLY ABUSED CHILDREN

Parents could not totally control the verbal and non-verbal cues which their children received:

> They were totally obsessed with lovers and willies. They were always drawing pictures of willies. They were so crude with the girls. They were always trying to shock them.

The impact of sexual abuse on other children was not merely confined to verbal communication. In 51 per cent of the placements some type of sexual activity was directed towards another child in the family. This included a wide range of behaviour: kissing other children open-mouthed; peering at them in the toilet; being obsessed with a baby's genitals; sexual play; touching; clawing; lying on top of other children sexually; inappropriate displaying of body; removing their own and other children's underclothes. Some parents were left with nagging doubts about the likelihood of these incidents escalating into more serious sexual episodes. Others worried that their children might enjoy the experience and want to imitate it with their peers. However, there was no indication of these fears being realised.

These events and incidents spurred families into action. A number used these opportunities to gather all the children around them and to teach them the rudimentary facts about relationships. Books on 'good' and 'bad' touching were useful aids. Many families perceived these events as having positive rather than negative consequences because they forced a new openness about sexual issues among all family members and opened up a quality of communication which had not previously been possible. Others struggled to know where they should begin. Sex education was difficult enough: now they were faced with having to find words and phrases to explain sexual abuse.

Certain groups of children were especially vulnerable. Children with disabilities were often singled out as targets for sexual advances. Generally they were good at safeguarding themselves. Even if they had inadequate speech, they were usually able to scream. Some families worried about babies who were too young to protect themselves. A number stated that they would never leave a baby alone with the abused child or relax their watchfulness even for a few minutes.

> She would want to change the shittiest nappy and at the first opportunity she would strip the baby off. She was obsessed with small children's private parts. She just could not be trusted.

32

There were extra risks associated with placing a number of sexually abused children together in the same family. When two children who had had very sexualised lifestyles were placed in close proximity a powerful sexual dynamic could be at work. In some instances foster children did manage to engage together sexually, causing distress for the foster family:

> I found Aaron (eight) in bed with another six-year-old foster girl. He said he was trying to 'screw' her. I asked the professionals, 'Can children have intercourse?' The answer I got was, 'We don't know.' All they could say was that she could not get pregnant.

There were also positive aspects associated with placing several abused children in the same family. One child talking about abuse helped to break the ice for others. Feelings of isolation were reduced. When a crisis erupted with one abused child it often helped to bring sensitive issues out into the open for other foster children. Some foster families admitted that they found it much easier to work collectively with a group of abused children rather than with an individual child. The group itself provided an immediate and spontaneous therapeutic situation.

Sibling placements brought some additional complexities to family life. The study comprised 14 sibling placements. In eight of these placements some type of sexual activity occurred between siblings. This included a range of behaviour from siblings masturbating together to efforts to engage in sexual intercourse. Siblings often engaged together sexually in the most blatant manner, regardless of whether they had an audience or not. This phenomenon inevitably involved other children as they witnessed these strange encounters and sometimes wanted to imitate them. These behaviour patterns were often difficult to break because they had been learned over prolonged periods. Practical steps had to be devised to monitor sibling relationships. Attempts were made to educate and re-educate them about relationships. The high level of anxiety evoked for families by the behaviour was illustrated by one family who installed baby alarms and two-way radios throughout their house.

Despite the degree of sexualised behaviour exhibited in families, sexual issues were by no means the ones which made the most profound impact on the other children. A more crucial issue was the fact that the abused child often absorbed so much parental time and energy that other children were pushed aside. Adoptive and foster parents often felt guilty about this. They were the first to acknowledge that it was hard for them to divide themselves evenly between all their children. Some made no secret of the fact that one practical outcome of parenting a sexually abused child was that their other children missed out on their attention and affection. A number of parents described their sense of weariness associated with the abused child's craving for attention and affection. These demands were exacerbated by the need to supervise all the abused child's activities to ensure that sexualised incidents did not escalate and to protect everyone from the risk of allegations of sexual abuse.

One difficult aspect which families had to face was when other children in the family began to copy the abused child's anti-social or disruptive behaviour. This did not seem to be a problem for natural children, but foster and adopted children who had been deprived themselves were exceptionally vulnerable. Violent temper tantrums, scraping wrists with razor blades, trying to carve names on arms and legs, and following another child's pattern of running away were just a few examples of problematic behaviour which were copied.

Positive factors for other children in the family were not easy to find. The toll on family life of re-parenting a sexually abused child extended beyond the adults in the family and affected the other children also. It was often a case of other children surviving despite the placement, because of their own inner resources, rather than thriving or finding fulfilment through the experience of having an abused child in their household.

Conclusions

This paper highlights a number of key issues in relation to the placement of sexually abused children in families. It underlines the importance of professionals obtaining the fullest possible background information on each child and of recognising the significance for the substitute family of knowing all the details about the abuse. Details which may seem minor can take on a whole new area of importance within the context of day-to-day living.

The need for partnership between professionals and substitute families is a well rehearsed principle. This study indicates that there is still much to be learned about putting this principle into practice. Concealing information about sexual abuse from substitute families or providing sparse information achieves nothing positive and merely places the abused child and members of the substitute family in an excessively vulnerable position.

It is unfair to expect substitute families to engage in this challenging task without adequate preparation and training. Social services departments and voluntary agencies need to consider how they can provide this for all prospective foster carers and adopters. As this study illustrates, any family could find themselves unexpectedly parenting a sexually abused child.

People need time to think about the powerful impact that sexual abuse is likely to have on them as individuals and on family relationships. This type of placement is likely to stir up sexual feelings, to trigger painful memories, to reawaken dormant feelings and to expose the most vulnerable areas of family life. Placements of abused children are likely to be interwoven with strong emotions such as anger, grief, disbelief, and guilt which inevitably affect day-to-day functioning. In particular, the trauma associated with the unnatural experience of sexual touching by an abused child has been mentioned. While there is a sense in which nothing can ever be quite as powerful as the real experience, several parents acknowledged that some type of psychological preparation for the impact of this experience would have been beneficial.

Re-parenting a sexually abused child involved re-educating the child to exchange inappropriate for appropriate behaviour. Faced with this complex task, it is unrealistic to expect substitute families to have an intuitive grasp of how to respond. Clear guidance is essential if substitute families are to avoid reinforcing unacceptable patterns of sexualised behaviour.

Other children in the family are vulnerable also. Even families who had thought beforehand about the likely effect on their own children acknowledged that the negative impact was much more subtle than they had ever anticipated. It was only too easy for the abused child to absorb a disproportionate amount of parental time so that minimal time remained for the other children. In this type of placement there is a constant danger that the abused child may thrive while other family members suffer. Substitute families need help on an emotional and practical level to ensure that the balance of family life is retained.

Once a sexually abused child joins a family, the issue of sex education cannot be brushed aside as irrelevant. If people struggle to discuss straightforward sex education within the family how are they going to explain sexual abuse? Indeed there is a sense in which the abused child's confusion can only be counteracted by the most explicit talking. These are issues which need to be examined with substitute families if they are going to be able to respond to the abused child's needs while at the same time helping their own children to grow through what is likely to be a very challenging experience for all the family members.

3 Working with children who have been sexually abused

John Fitzgerald

John Fitzgerald has had a long career in child care as practitioner, manager, trainer and writer. He is the founding director of the inter-disciplinary consultation agency The Bridge, which is frequently consulted in cases involving sexual abuse. In this chapter he concentrates on work after disclosure, describing an evaluation system that considers children in the context of the whole experience, suggesting how they and their parents can be involved positively in such work and summarising the range of techniques and specialisms available.

Introduction

Child sexual abuse is not a new topic; it has been with us from time immemorial. It is only in the last five years, however, that it has become a topic in the public domain in the UK. In some other parts of the world, for instance in the United States, it has been a 'hot' subject for much longer. Whatever stage we are in, however, there is no doubt that this subject causes more anxiety, concern and heated debate than any other in the field of child care.

To date, with few exceptions, the focus in the UK has been almost entirely upon detection and ways of enabling children to disclose abuse. This was epitomised by the events in Cleveland during 1987.[1] In the concern to 'rescue' children little has been done to devise systematic post-disclosure services for the young victims of sexual abuse.

Children and young people who have been abused do not cease to have needs after they have disclosed abuse and it is to this area of work that I believe we should be directing our efforts over the next five years. In the United States there is now movement towards recognition of the longer term needs of such children and, in the wake of this movement, the beginnings of the means to meet those needs.

In this paper I want to consider six basic areas:

– the philosophical stance

- evaluation systems
- the availability of direct work techniques
- inter-disciplinary participation
- involving the child
- parental involvement

The philosophical stance

Following the events in Cleveland, there was a rush to provide services for the victims of sexual abuse, mainly focusing on the abuse and its immediate effects. Indeed, it could have been termed 'jumping on the band-wagon'. This is not unusual, of course, when what appears to be a new need is uncovered in the field of child care.

However, in The Bridge, we have found that children and young people in this situation have needs which usually go well beyond ending the sexual abuse to which they have been subjected. Focusing solely on the abuse ignores the fact that many such children may have been subjected to a range of other abuses or damaging experiences in some cases as severe as the sexual abuse. These are children who have been neglected physically and emotionally or who have been physically or emotionally, as well as sexually, abused. In our experience, one or other of these conditions has always been present where we have been asked to help with sexually abused children. In some cases serious health issues have also emerged. I believe it to be misguided, therefore, to attempt to treat only the effects of sexual abuse and leave untreated other areas which can lead to just as many difficulties for the child in the future.

In fact, the very effects of our intervention at the disclosure stage can add to the child's difficulties. For example, if the alleged abuser is one of the parents then there is every possibility that the child may be separated from one or both parents so that, at the moment of what is seen as 'rescue', the effects of separation and loss are added to the child's already painful experience.

I would argue therefore that, in trying to define ways of working with children and young people who have been sexually abused, we need to be very clear that we have a responsibility to provide services for children that are based on their whole experience, not just the experience of sexual abuse. In so doing we should ensure that carers have a full and balanced picture of the children and their needs from the outset.

Evaluation systems

If we are to be of any use to children, our work must be prefaced by a systematic *evaluation* of their needs. Assessment services can range from a brief and cursory discussion in the community to a full hospital-based psychological assessment, with many different systems in between.

The importance of clear and systematic evaluation of the needs of children and young people is not peculiar to those who have been sexually abused; it is one of the major services still not effectively available for many children and young people in care. *Protecting children*, published by the Department of Health,[2] is a useful aid to practitioners and managers charged with the responsibility of assessing the needs of children and young people. The Bridge operates, as a central point of its service, a systematic evaluation model which can be used to help workers in effective evaluation of need. This analyses components of an assessment system and how the system can be used in planning.

It is important that each area of the child's life is considered before any attempt is made to devise a programme of work. A thorough evaluation should eliminate confusion over the causes that lie behind children's behaviour. Many severely deprived children, whether or not sexually abused, display behaviour in seeking adult attention that may be perceived as sexually provocative in that they attempt to achieve physical contact. For example, Emma, a three-year-old grossly neglected throughout her babyhood, greeted her male social worker at their first meeting by running across the room, grabbing him around a thigh and rubbing herself against him. There was no question of sexual abuse in her history but she was desperate for human contact and took hold of that part of him available to a very small girl. The social worker's immediate experience, however, was of a sexual approach. When he picked her up and held her at eye level he could experience her simply as a child.

Emma and children like her, whether girls or boys, are particularly vulnerable to sexual abuse. The quality of life that they have experienced has affected their development so that they may overcompensate for earlier loss, or have perhaps become 'stuck' at a much earlier age, with its accompanying behaviour. These children should be protected from potential abusers and it should be made clear to those working with them, especially carers, that they may provoke sexual responses.

I believe that the areas to be covered in an evaluation are:

– a detailed chronological history of the child's experiences including numbers and changes of carer and levels of physical and emotional care

– a full health and developmental history

– a detailed history of the child's educational experience

– full details of the circumstances and type of abuse experienced by the child or young person

– a record of the child's own views and perspectives in relation to his or her own life, and how this was obtained

– a record of the parental views and perspectives, including the parent who may be the abuser, and how this was obtained

– a clear plan for the future.

Time spent on consideration of these areas can pay handsome dividends when devising a treatment programme. Even the most experienced carers are inevitably inhibited in their attempts to help children when gaps exist in this vital planning stage.

Availability of direct work techniques

In preparing a treatment programme, there is a risk that we may assume that we have to devise new techniques to help the child or young person. However, if our evaluation has examined the whole child, we shall find that many of our techniques used in other areas of child care work are equally applicable here.

Life work with a child is now increasingly accepted as part of preparation for placement in a new family. By this I mean helping the child to look at the chronology of their life and at their feelings about their whole history to date, thus helping to develop a positive sense of self. To achieve that goal, many creative methods are available such as waterplay, use of clay, use of life maps, flow charts, art work, drama, music, puppets, stories – the list is endless. Alongside these techniques, the worker must develop a strong working relationship with the child or young person. The techniques, in fact, depend for success upon the ability of the worker to use the relationship as a treatment tool. Indeed, in some situations the establishment of a therapeutic relationship may be an objective in itself.

Other life work examples involve helping children to learn about their own bodies and the boundaries governing the behaviour of adults and children. Exploring these areas tends to be seen as specific to children who have been sexually abused, but I would argue that they are equally applicable to work with children who have been damaged by separation. Learning about appropriate and inappropriate touching is also essential here, as so many children have suffered from distortion in this area of their lives which is, in itself, abuse.

Neither should we ignore the racial, cultural and religious context within which a child lives. Far too often these issues are not given sufficient weight by white workers. The Afro-Caribbean Educational Resource Centre produce some beautiful material[3] which, though originally designed for use in schools, is readily adaptable to other settings.

Groupwork is helpful for some children or young people. Such an approach may be of particular benefit to youngsters who have poor peer relationships or where the sexual abuse occurred within paedophile rings.

It is not enough just to pick a technique at random; I believe it is important to select methods carefully with which both the child or young person and the worker can feel comfortable. Most carers possess natural gifts of communication with children and many devise their own techniques, but they may need help in focusing their work and should always be offered consultation and support. Work methods should also be selected in the context of the child's identified needs. Sexual abuse has a unique meaning to each of the abused individuals, and chosen methods of work must reflect that uniqueness.

Inter-disciplinary participation

When child sexual abuse occurs, the primary responsibility for the case rests with the social services or social work department. But the resources that are available outside the department are often neglected. Social workers who can carry out skilled direct work with the child or young person may not be available, so sometimes a specialist worker must join the team to provide additional skills. It is important that this individual is drawn into the team and does not work in isolation. Specialists from other disciplines can be of great help also, such as child psychiatrists, psychologists, psychotherapists and art, drama, music and play therapists. Indeed, one of the most skilled people in working with children and young people that I have met is an occupational therapist. We often have stereotyped views of the services that differing therapists provide, so that often no one thinks of approaching them to assist in one particular case.

The Bridge has an advisory group made up of representatives from these disciplines. When we set it up, we asked each member of the group as a first task to share something of their work with the rest. In the ensuing discussion, we were all surprised to discover just how far our individual methods overlapped with those of colleagues from other disciplines. For example, it is not unusual for a drama therapist to use music or for a music therapist to use art or for an art therapist to use techniques that an occupational therapist might use.

It is clear that, while within these disciplines there is a high degree of specialist knowledge, there is also a great deal of common experience. So, when trying to determine how to use an outside specialist, we should first identify what it is that we are asking the specialist to do and then select someone who can provide that service from the range of disciplines available to us. Carers' involvement in these decisions is essential, since their support is required throughout if the work is to achieve its end.

The Bridge is composing a computerised resource index including, amongst other things, details of various specialists available to work with children and young people. We hope eventually to be able to extend this beyond our own use on a trial basis.

Involving the child
It seems extraordinary that, although since 1976 it has been a statutory requirement that the views and wishes of children in care should be taken into account when making plans for them, often only lip service is paid to this requirement. Not only is it good practice to involve children in this way, it is their *right* to be involved in decision making about their future. So it is with children and young people

who have been sexually abused.

I am not one of those who subscribe to the view that all children in all circumstances should attend x, y, and z meetings, case conferences and reviews. For some, it is a frightening prospect to be faced by all those professionals, most of whom will talk in jargon. (Perhaps we need a paper on how to 'de-jargonise' discussion at case conferences and reviews.) That, however, does not preclude us from ensuring that a true reflection of their views, wishes and ideas are included in our deliberations. Listening to carers who listen to children over long periods will often help to achieve this aim.

This applies equally to the way we present a treatment programme. Why should such a programme be imposed? Should there not be an early opportunity for a child or young person to express their views on our proposals? Sometimes, however, in order truly to understand their views and wishes, we have to move away from verbal interviews with direct questions and into the creative areas of communication that have been discussed earlier. Some young people find it extremely difficult to express what may be deep, painful thoughts and views. This does not make their contribution any less valid and their difficulties should be taken into account in the overall decision-making process and the long-term programme of work.

It is equally important to recognise that some young people do not wish to disclose that they have been sexually abused or share their feelings in words. Sometimes we may have to accept their silence whilst at other times the use of creative techniques over a long period may enable them to communicate. We have estimated that some 15 per cent of young people on referral to The Bridge had been sexually abused, many of them only sharing that information years after the event.

Sometimes adulthood arrives before young people can talk about abuse. While in care there may not have been any obvious place they could feel comfortable enough to ask for help. We do not have a right to 'force' a disclosure but rather to be responsive to a young person's needs. Whilst this may create conflict for professionals and carers in balancing the requirements of the law against the needs of the child, our responsibility is to meet the needs of our client, the child.

Parental involvement
Working with children who need therapeutic help will be of little use

if we exclude their parents. The child who has been sexually abused may well have suffered the loss of one parent, but that does not mean that the parent should be excluded inevitably from their child's life or from assisting in helping the child to overcome the traumas experienced. At best the child will have suffered a breach of trust and a damaged attachment, and will experience guilt feelings, thinking that what happened was their fault. Parents who have abused their children can, in some cases, help an agency to deal with some of these issues.

It may be appropriate to continue with supervised contact and to involve an abusing parent in trying to contain the damage done to the relationship. It might also be appropriate for an abusing parent to assist in trying to reduce the guilt which a child or young person is feeling. I am not, of course, advocating the wholesale involvement of abusing parents without clearly thought out functions and controls. I am, however, advocating recognition that there may well be circumstances in which abusing parents can and ought to help in the work that is being undertaken.

When an abusing parent does remain involved, consideration should be given to the feelings of the child's carers and other workers close to the child. These feelings, understandably, may be intensely hostile; they may include disgust and even revulsion. Such feelings, if repressed, could resurface at a time when future family relationships are in the balance. Confronting them at an early stage could prevent disaster later.

The non-abusing parent, too, usually has a major part to play in the direct work programme that we attempt. It is folly to assume that, because a child has been sexually abused, only professionals can help the child. Children and young people do not deserve such arrogance. Other than in exceptional circumstances, non-abusing parents must be involved, but they may need considerable help themselves in order to deal with their own pain.

The Bridge has a work programme designed for use when we have identified the needs of the child or young person. We take one chart for each need identified and then set out the objectives, techniques, timescales, method of monitoring, key people and other factors that may impinge on the programme of work.

Such programmes should integrate the needs of both children and their families. Set out on pages 45 and 46 are two completed work

WORK
PROGRAMME   Child's name   Sarah   Date of birth   7.4.78

Child's needs	Suggested work programme	Time-scale and monitoring	Key people	Support, resource and policy issues
Life work: • to understand chronology and feelings about life to date • to help deal with guilt feelings about sexual abuse and family disintegration • to begin building a positive sense of self • to introduce mother into an understanding of Sarah's life	**Stage 1** • Use of loving and caring waterplay • Use of puppets to act out story • Use of art therapy sessions **Stage 2** • Making a detailed frieze (flow chart) of life to date • Making a life map of numerous geographic moves • Use of art therapy sessions **Stage 3** • Introduce mother into programme, at appropriate points in Sarah's story	• Weekly sessions of one hour, initially, for six months and then to be reviewed • Monthly meeting of key people to discuss progress • To be phased in with remainder of programme	• Sarah • Birth mother • Art therapist • Social worker • Team leader (to chair monitoring meetings)	• Will department provide financial resources for art therapy? • Will department provide suitably equipped location for all work to be done? • For staff undertaking new work, will department provide opportunity to practise techniques in advance, as well as provide professional supervision? • Will time be made available for staff to undertake the work?

WORK PROGRAMME

Child's name Sarah

Date of birth 7.4.78

Child's needs	Suggested work programme	Time-scale and monitoring	Key people	Support, resource and policy issues
Return to birth mother: • to repair damaged trust and attachment • to provide confidence in each other • to familiarise mother and Sarah with living together again	**Stage 1** • Involve mother in all facets of programme • Devise touching exercise for both to re-establish contact and set boundaries **Stage 2** • Develop access to the point of Sarah's spending increasing time at home with mother • Sarah's move home **Stage 3** • Provision of intensive social work support	• To be phased in with remainder of work programme and to be reviewed after six months • Monthly progress meetings to monitor work	• Sarah • Birth mother • Art therapist • Social worker • Team leader (to chair monitoring meetings)	• Will time be made available for staff to undertake work? • Will mother be rehoused in time? • Will sufficient additional financial resources be made available to assist mother?

programme charts, designed in respect of a 12-year-old girl who had been sexually abused over a seven-year period by her birth mother's boyfriend. Sarah, as I will call her, who was living in a residential setting, was to return to her mother and the programme was designed to help both of them learn to live together.

A similar approach was adopted with the other identified needs, as follows:

- separation and loss – to help both Sarah and her mother cope with the effects of separation from a number of people, partly as a result of the sexual abuse

- attachment work – to help Sarah develop a clear idea of what is realistic and to help her mother to understand Sarah's emotional needs

- health – to investigate fully Sarah's potential hearing difficulties

- education – to provide a statement of special needs under the terms of the 1981 Education Act to deal with specific learning difficulties identified during earlier evaluation.

There is no magic in writing programmes in this way, but their advantages include:

- ensuring that all who are associated with the child or young person are moving in the same direction

- providing a tool or checklist for monitoring the progress of the programme

- providing a tool or checklist for use in supervision and support of the staff involved in the programme. I would add that no one should attempt this sort of programme without very clear and competent professional support and supervision.

Conclusion
The key areas then that I want to emphasise are as follows:

that children and young people are seen as such, first and foremost, and that where sexual abuse has occurred it is but one part, albeit a very significant part, of their lives

- that in trying to provide services for children and young people and undertaking direct work with them we are conscious of all the needs they may have, not just those which are related to sexual abuse

- that we are aware of the very wide range of disciplines that can assist us, and more importantly, assist the children and young people involved

- that we are clear that both abusing and non-abusing parents often have a significant part to play in any treatment programme that we devise

- that we do not penalise the non-abusing parent by excluding them inappropriately, which in turn may penalise their child

- that no one, whether social worker, carer or therapist should work with a child in isolation – consultation and support *must* be made available

- that the child or young person, as a right, should be enabled to contribute their views, their wishes and their ideas both to planning and to direct work in a form and within a time-scale appropriate to their needs.

References

1   Butler Sloss E *Report of the inquiry into child abuse in Cleveland* (The Cleveland Report) HMSO, 1987.

2   *Protecting children: a guide for social workers undertaking a comprehensive assessment* Department of Health, HMSO, 1988.

3   *I'm special myself: resource pack* 1987: Afro-Caribbean Education Resource Centre, Wyvil School, Wyvil Road, London SW8 2TJ.

Useful reading

Bryer M *Planning in child care: a guide for team leaders and their teams* BAAF, 1988.

Dale P, Davies P, Morrison T and Waters J *Dangerous families: assessment and treatment of child abuse* Tavistock Publications, 1986.

Oaklander V *Windows to our children* Utah: Real People Press, 1978.

Planning for children Family Rights Group, 1988.

Porter R (ed) *Child sexual abuse within the family* Tavistock Publications, 1984.

Ryan T and Walker R *Making life story books* BAAF, 1985.

Social work decisions in child care: recent research findings and their implications DHSS, HMSO, 1985.

Working together: a guide to arrangements for inter-agency cooperation for the protection of children from abuse Department of Health, 1988.

Children's books and materials

Aggarwal and Fairclough *I am* series (ie Muslim, Rastafarian) Franklyn Watts Books.

Astrop J *My secret file* Puffin, 1989.

Hindley and Rawson *How your body works* Usborne Publishing, 1975.

Kaufman J *All about us* Hamlyn, 1974.

Lift and see (puzzle) Show and Tell Dolls, 1989.

Maxime J E *Black like me* (Workbooks 1 and 2) Emani Publications, 1987.

Thom M and Macliver C *Bruce's story* The Children's Society, 1986.

Resources and training

Intervening in child sexual abuse audio tapes, University of Glasgow.

In touch with children training pack, BAAF, 1984.

Working with sexually abused children: resource pack for professionals The Children's Society.

Further information on training materials is available from the Training Advisory Resource for Child Sexual Abuse (TAGOSAC) at the National Children's Bureau, 8 Wakley Street, London EC1V 7QE.

4 The medical contribution

Marion Miles

Dr Marion Miles is a consultant community paediatrician in an inner London area, medical adviser to both statutory and voluntary agencies and a long-standing member of the BAAF Medical Group. This chapter outlines the role of the medical examination in the treatment of abused children and identifies some health issues that may arise from a child's previous history, at the examination or afterwards in the course of work with a child.

Introduction

The carers of sexually abused children should routinely be given comprehensive information about the health and developmental status of the children in their care. In many cases a health issue may be very much to the fore and may, as in sexual abuse, constitute the major reason for alternative care. In other cases health problems may be identified during the course of getting to know the child. Whatever the individual circumstances, the carer should at all times have easy access to a named doctor who is identified when the placement commences and is readily available to give or obtain specialist advice.

This paper discusses the different health issues which need to be considered and the ways in which they may be identified, and summarises the sources of health support available.

Seeing the doctor

It is unlikely that the diagnosis of child sexual abuse will be proved on the basis of physical findings obtained during the medical examination. In the majority of cases there are no abnormal physical signs. Even so, the medical examination has an important part to play and, unless there are exceptional circumstances, the child considered to have been sexually abused will have been examined.

The examination should never be hurried but taken at a pace dictated by the child who should be supported and reassured by the presence of a trusted adult, usually the mother. A full general examination is undertaken which leaves inspection of the genital and anal areas to the end. More intrusive procedures such as the taking of swabs may also be necessary. However, since ideally and usually the examination is performed by a doctor who is skilled in looking at, playing with and talking to children, in friendly, comfortable and private surroundings which encourage the relaxation of the child and parents, there should be little upset and no lasting reluctance 'to see the doctor' again.

Increasingly the examination is undertaken by a paediatrician and a police surgeon who work together so that a joint opinion can be formed thereby avoiding the need for repeated medical examinations. Depending on the age and the wishes of the child or young person, consideration may have to be given to the sex of the medical examiner(s).

It is very important to encourage a child who has been exposed to abuse to view visits to the doctor with enthusiasm rather than fear. Unfortunately, many children are still threatened by their parents with medical contact as punishment for difficult behaviour or some other problem rather as policemen were used in the past. Even when the reference is not so negative, parents often create an unnecessarily unsympathetic atmosphere by ushering the child into the doctor's room with the remark, 'Don't worry, the doctor's not going to hurt you'!

Since there are many situations when sexually abused children will need a continuing medical input after the abuse, their carers may find that they have to invent novel and enterprising ways of enhancing the doctor-child contact. Obviously the doctor will have to work at this relationship also. Clearly both the doctor and the carers need to have some information about the events preceding the examination in order to reassure the child appropriately. In some cases this information can be sensitively shared using the information for foster carers whereby the child's health and health care is recorded by the agency's medical adviser.

The medical examination which is undertaken in cases of child sexual abuse covers many areas. During the process of the examination a history will have been taken and recorded and the general health, growth and development assessed. At the same time any signs of abuse will have been noted. As a result of the examination the need for treatment, perhaps for an injury or an infection, may have been identified. The history may alert the doctor to some other problem or reveal the omission of some aspect of the surveillance programme recommended for all children. Any one of these factors, or a combination of several, may mean that there is a need for a continuing medical input. Other conditions, which may or may not have a physical basis, can arise following abuse and they will also require medical consultation. Some of the different types of health problems, their presentation, identification and treatment will be considered below in greater detail.

Health issues arising from the history
Child sexual abuse may result in an exacerbation of a chronic illness which had previously become stable or controlled by treatment. Examples include asthma, epilepsy and diabetes. Removal of the abuse may result in regained control but a review of treatment, including medication and diet, may be necessary. Soiling and wetting may occur and may be directly related to the abuse. Night wetting is common and occurs in at least ten per cent of all five-year-old children. Wetting by day may have an emotional basis but its presence means that a urinary tract infection should be excluded before ascribing it to a behavioural change. Soiling may be associated with constipation and, even when it is the direct result of abuse, may take a long time to resolve. Treatment may require the co-ordination of a paediatric input with that of a psychiatrist, psychologist or psychotherapist.

An abused child may present with a history of developmental problems or deterioration in school work. An overview of development is obtained during the examination undertaken during the investigation of child sexual abuse. However, a fully comprehensive developmental assessment cannot, for obvious reasons, be attempted at that time. When there are indications that a full assessment is appropriate this will need to be arranged as a follow-up procedure, usually on a multi-disciplinary basis. The effect of emotional abuse in these children may be greatest on language development which is especially vulnerable. Although it may improve dramatically on cessation of the abuse the advice of a speech therapist may reassure the carers that appropriate language stimulation is being offered. The history may reveal that the preventive aspects of good child health have lapsed. Thus the immunisation programme for the child concerned may have fallen behind and needs to be brought up to date. In the upheaval and distress which surround the diagnosis of sexual abuse, immunisation uptake may be given a low priority. There may be an understandable reluctance to inflict 'jabs' on the child but it would be misplaced kindness to deny or delay the protection offered by a vaccination programme.

Health issues identified during examination

Children who have been sexually abused may also have been physically abused. In a survey of sexual abuse in the UK 15 per cent of the cases were associated with physical abuse.[1] The physical injuries may be in the genital or anal areas only or they may be more widely spread over the body including the mouth. Injuries range from scratches, bruises, abrasions, bites, burns, and scalds to damage to bones.

Depending on the degree of physical injury, immediate treatment may have been necessary. Fortunately, most of the injuries heal spontaneously although burns and bony injuries in particular may require more specific treatment.

Happily bowel upset following anal abuse is uncommon. Anal fissures may demand attention but reassurance can be given that it is most unlikely that there will be any permanent damage. Follow-up examination is usually recommended both to check that healing is taking place and to reinforce the message that 'all is well'.

A history of irritation in the anal or genital area associated with soreness and scratching may alert the doctor to look for evidence of threadworms. If worm infestation occurs in conjunction with sexual abuse it will need to be treated appropriately. Poor hygiene may cause redness and soreness or a napkin rash in younger children. Inflammation of the vulval area, resulting in a variable amount of discharge, is not uncommon in girls who have not been abused. Frequently there is no clear cause for the condition and swabs are negative. Sometimes the discharge is associated with poor hygiene or the use of disinfectants or bubble bath substances. It may be due to threadworm infestation, it may be part of a generalised infection or, very rarely, it may be caused by the presence of a foreign body. In these cases appropriate treatment will be necessary. When a child has been sexually abused the discharge may be due to infection by sexually transmitted disease. It has been suggested that up to 13 per cent of sexually abused children are found to be infected in this way.[2]

Although it is considered to be good practice to screen sexually abused children for such infection, and essential in cases of stranger abuse, it has to be remembered that symptoms may not develop for a long time. Infection may involve the rectum, throat or urethra as well as the vulva or vagina and may be caused by one or more of the particular bacteria, viruses or other organisms concerned.

Since the incubation period for different sexually transmitted diseases varies it may not be appropriate to rely on swabs taken at the initial medical examination for identification and diagnosis. Follow-up examination to ensure that swabs and blood samples are taken at the correct time is essential and treatment will depend upon the findings.

Transmission of HIV infection as a result of sexual abuse is rare but is likely to increase. The need for counselling and blood screening has to be considered carefully in individual cases using the relevant services.

When abuse occurs in post-pubertal girls there may be a need to exclude pregnancy. Subsequent action will depend upon individual circumstances. Immediate treatment may include the use of 'morning after' therapy. Abortion counselling may need to be arranged if the abuse occurred less recently.

At some point during the medical examination, measurements of the child's height and weight are recorded. Some children who have been exposed to emotional abuse and neglect will have also suffered physical or sexual abuse. The outcome of longstanding emotional abuse may be the stunting of growth due to deficient secretion of growth hormone.

In this situation, when the height measurement is plotted on a growth chart the child will be found to be unacceptably small or to be growing at an unacceptably slow rate. When examined the child's body proportions show relatively short legs while siblings and parents are of average size and proportion.

Often there is a history of disordered eating patterns. This may include the stealing of food, the ransacking of dustbins, the eating of unusual substances and gorging if allowed to eat freely. Not surprisingly these unhappy children show other behavioural problems which include deliberate wetting and the smearing of faeces.

When the abuse ceases the production of growth hormone improves and the child grows dramatically within months. Follow-up with careful growth checks is necessary to ensure that the expected accelerated growth has taken place and has been maintained. If the expected improvement is not demonstrated organic disorders for the failure to thrive have to be excluded.

While acknowledging that all abuse involves some emotional ill-treatment it seems possible that emotional abuse and sexual abuse co-exist more commonly than previously recognised.

Development

Sexual abuse may be suspected because of changes in manner, attitude, demeanour, or behaviour which in turn affect the development of a young child or the school performance of an older one. Sexual abuse and emotional abuse co-exist and overlap. When sexual abuse is associated with an unrewarding, unstimulating environment a young child's development is likely to be adversely affected. The different parameters of development do not usually show the same degree of problem, however, and motor development is less likely to be affected than those skills which require contact, interaction and personal encouragement, namely language and reasoning.

A base-line assessment of ability should be made by a paediatrician who has a special interest in development so that progress can be monitored. Such an assessment should involve other professionals such as a clinical psychologist or speech therapist when necessary. If there is delay of language development then it is essential to consider whether there is a hearing problem. If this cannot be easily excluded then a more detailed assessment of hearing may be indicated which in turn may suggest the need for surgical or other treatment. Many children have intermittent middle ear problems, often referred to as 'glue ear', which affect the ability to listen and to hear but which improve with time. In most cases, given parental understanding of the problem and appropriate care, no specific treatment is required. However, if such a child who cannot hear properly is underestimated and abused, it is not surprising that language development suffers.

A more severe delay of language development may require advice on more intensive treatment from a speech therapist. In most cases the restoration of a caring, stimulating environment will result in a striking and satisfying improvement.

Learning

The notification of children under five years of age who are likely to have learning problems at school, and who will need special educational help, is usually the responsibility of a child health doctor acting on behalf of the health authority. Some children who have been abused may not have had their early progress monitored through a child health surveillance programme offered by a general practitioner or the community child health service. Thus the possibility of there being educational problems may not have been considered before being examined at the time of the abuse. Regardless of whether the learning problem(s) are associated with abuse or coincidental, a comprehensive assessment of needs, preferably at a child development centre, may be appropriate. Arrangements can then be made, on a multi-disciplinary basis, to ensure that the child receives the support and schooling which is needed depending on his or her age.

Children of school age who have been exposed to sexual abuse may show deterioration of their school work associated with poor concentration. Again any health reasons which might account for poor progress have to be excluded so that the school, possibly with the advice of an educational psychologist or specialist teacher, can provide the appropriate support. Older children who have been involved in sexual abuse may resort to the use of glue, alcohol or other drugs. Treatment is difficult and may need collaboration between a psychologist or psychiatrist and a doctor experienced in adolescent medicine.

Later presenting health issues

Mind or body?

In the upheaval which usually surrounds the diagnosis and confirmation of child sexual abuse, psychosomatic symptoms may not have been considered or identified or they may have become quiescent. After placement with carers pre-existing or new symptoms may emerge. There is a range of complaints which may occur and they include soiling, wetting, abdominal pains, headaches and disturbances of eating patterns. An organic basis for these symptoms may be present and will need to be excluded by medical consultation and possible investigation before psychiatric or psychological treatment is introduced.

Anxieties
Anxiety about the nature of any physical damage incurred and its long-term effects may be expressed by an abused child. In these cases a follow-up medical examination is particularly relevant. It can be constructively reassuring and can play a significant part in the process of recovery.

Other anxieties which may arise include the risk of sexually transmitted disease, HIV infection and possible adverse effects on the child's own sexual activity and fulfilment. Again, counselling, examination and investigation may, in different combinations, be relevant and necessary. At all times, the aim and intention should be to reassure the child and to restore his or her self-image. Although all efforts to avoid unnecessary and repetitive medical examinations should be made, there are many occasions when it will be appropriate. Omission of an examination, or acceptance in a negative manner, would not serve the child's best interest. Support from the carer in these circumstances is invaluable.

Sources of health support
There are many health professionals who are available to provide support for carers of sexually abused children. The range of psychiatric and psychological support is described elsewhere.

The general practitioner leads the primary care team. Specialist medical advice is available from hospital or community paediatricians. Depending upon the problems encountered, consultants in other specialities may need to be involved. For children under five the community child health doctor, working in a child health clinic or advising a day nursery, is available to provide support and advice, while for older children the school doctor may be more appropriate.

The nursing services have a valuable contribution to make. The health visitor can relate to the general practitioner and clinic doctor while the school nurse can liaise with the general practitioner, school doctor or educational staff.

Thus there are many areas in which a medical contribution can be made to the support for carers of sexually abused children. There are, potentially, many different doctors available to give that support. Most importantly the medical contribution must be, and be seen to be, fully integrated with any support provided by other agencies.

References

1   Hobbs C and Wynne J 'Child sexual abuse' *Lancet* ii, 1987.

2   *Sexually abused children* Royal Society of Medicine Booklet, 1988.

5 Support from the educational services

Renuka Jeyarajah Dent

Renuka Jeyarajah Dent is an educational psychologist in the inner London area and until 1987 was the first black issues project worker at BAAF. She describes here the structure in schools for pastoral and emotional care, which must be seen against the background of the school's primary function, that is, to teach children. She considers the teacher's role in supporting abused children by describing good practice that can be expected in every school. Specific examples of good practice in the areas of prevention, identification and work with abused children are not the focus of this chapter, although the urgent need for training to enable teachers to work in these areas is highlighted.

Introduction

Surveys in Britain[1] suggest that one in ten children are the victims of some form of sexual abuse. Exact numbers are difficult to obtain because of the different definitions of child sexual abuse and the stigma associated with it. Children from all social classes, races and cultures can be victims of abuse.

In Britain, every child between the age of five and 16 years has a legal right to education. Teachers are the only people outside the family to have almost daily contact with children. In school, teachers are *in loco parentis*, that is, they exercise the duties of a parent not only to promote the general welfare and safety of a child but also to refrain from abuse and ill-treatment. They have no statutory power over the children, but as citizens possess rights and duties with regard to them.

Teachers have basic training in child psychology, child developmental behaviour and child health. They can observe and describe children in the context of other children and are thus well placed to identify problems that may point to abuse and to initiate assessment. This is their 're-active' role in relation to abuse. Schools can also take a 'pro-active' role by trying, through the curriculum, to influence future parenting in young people and even current parenting through home-school link units or similar projects. There has been an increase recently in the availability of material to help children understand that they have a right to say 'no' to interference, and to speak out about it. There is still controversy as to whether programmes aiming to empower children will disturb them, force them out of innocence too early or make them unduly anxious, suspicious or frightened of people close to them. It is not the purpose of this paper to enter into this discussion, but schools must attempt to convey the message that all children are of value despite experiences that may have threatened their self-esteem. Children should know that they are dependent on the adults around them and that they cannot be blamed for some events.

Children with special needs

A teacher's primary task is to enable children to learn. Local education authorities have a statutory obligation to meet the educational needs of children within their areas. Teachers are not instructed in 'how to teach the sexually abused child'. This is as it should be. Abused children are children under stress. They are children whose self-esteem has been affected and this can cause them to react in a multitude of ways. They may present with behavioural difficulties, physical symptoms such as stomach pain, relationship problems, lack of progress in reading, poor concentration, and so on. They will react in many different ways and checklists of 'symptoms' and risk factors, although providing useful guidelines,[2] could be misleading. What is important is that children's needs are seen in context.

Schools are used to dealing with children who have special needs. The Warnock Report[3] indicates that about one in five children will need extra help at some point in their school life. One in ten children will have a longer-lasting need for special education requiring further assessment and sometimes a formal, detailed profile of their needs. The Education Act 1981 replaced the 11 categories of handicap defined in the Education Act 1944 with the concept of 'special educational need'. This embraces all factors which have a bearing on a child's educational progress. No longer are children seen simply in terms of a label – in the present case: 'sexually abused'.

Schools have a duty to deliver the curriculum to children. They will also be aware of the needs of the community they serve. Poverty, poor housing and unemployment can give rise to problems that directly affect schools, such as violence, apathy and racism. These problems can, of course, also arise in more affluent areas that have their own stress factors. The pressure to provide an adequate pastoral as well as educational service in schools may sometimes seem overwhelming (especially in state schools, with the demands of the national curriculum), but a good school realises that the well-being of each child is best served by aiming to achieve the well-being of the whole school, staff and children alike. There will be a continuum of needs in the children requiring a range of approaches to meet them and to enable the children to learn. Schools are organised so that staff can support each other and at the same time have access to professionals outside the school who can offer a service. This is important if flexibility in methods of delivering the curriculum is to be achieved. Some children will however, inevitably, fall outside the range that the school can cater for.

Support available within the education system
In a *secondary school*, each child is known directly or indirectly to a number of adults. The diagram below illustrates the kind of support structure offered to a child at a school. The titles given to the adults vary, for instance in Scotland the form tutor and head of year are called 'guidance teacher' and 'head of guidance' respectively.

Normal pastoral support for the individual child[+]

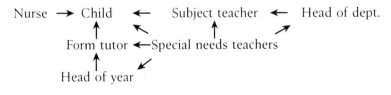

This system will be supported further by senior teachers or department heads. The adults in the diagram function as follows:

School nurse	discusses health problems with the child and monitors any progress
	deals with first aid
	acts as an informal counsellor (sometimes it is an advantage not being a teacher)

Form tutor	knows the pupil well communicates with the parents helps with personal adjustment and any problems arising
Head of year	supports the tutor should know the child often is the person who deals in the first place with outside agencies
Heads of departments	support teachers both in preparation of curriculum materials and in methods of delivery
Special needs teachers	advise subject staff and heads of departments on curriculum materials and methods of approach. Support tutors and heads of year with any problems arising and make, if necessary, special provision for the child either by working in the classroom alongside the subject teacher or by withdrawal of the child for small group teaching.

In a *primary school*, the children meet with fewer adults, their class teacher often having direct contact with the head teacher. There is always a member of staff with responsibility for special needs. There will usually be links between a secondary school and its feeder primary schools.

Teachers have always monitored children's progress and the national curriculum makes this a formal requirement. If a child is not learning or there is some other reason for concern and the resources of the school fail to achieve the desired effect, advice will be sought from specialists outside the school. Examples of such staff are:

Education welfare officers Education social workers	can sometimes provide an expertise similar to social workers in social services departments. They do not have statutory powers to the same extent, but can have statutory powers to ensure attendance[5]
Educational psychologists	have a knowledge of the emotional, psychological and intellectual development of children and of parent-child relationships. They have experience in teaching as well as in psychology

School medical officers	qualified doctors who visit schools to ensure that medical aspects of a child's development are considered. They will alert the school to any health factors which may affect learning. The frequency of their visits depends upon their health authority.

Any concerns at school should be discussed fully with the child's parents or carers and permission must be obtained before referral is made to professionals outside the school. Sometimes, however, the school has a statutory duty to involve other professionals, for instance in the case of non-attendance or actual/suspected abuse. It is the responsibility of key teachers and medical staff to develop a tradition of communication with parents through normal school activities so that this can be put to positive use if problems arise. A special effort may have to be made to link with the carer when a child has had a change of schools.

Referrals for specialist help

If a child is not progressing, despite the provision available, the Education Act 1981 allows for the *formal educational assessment* of a child's needs. The psychologist, school doctor and teachers must contribute to this and other professionals involved with the child will do so too. This enables the child's educational needs to be investigated and specified in a *statement of special educational needs*. The local education authority can then plan to meet these needs. They may do this, for example, by the provision of extra staff at the school or by recommending a smaller, more specialised educational setting. Provision varies with each authority, but the views of the child's carers are always considered. Statements have to be reviewed annually and again formally at around the child's thirteenth year.

Schools will use the resources and mechanisms available to them to enable a child to learn. For a sexually abused child there may be the active involvement of a social worker or therapist. Child guidance and child and family psychiatry units are also available. These provide a multi-disciplinary child psychiatric assessment, and therapeutic and advisory services in the community. Generally, referrals are accepted from professionals and families alike, but in the case of sexual abuse it is particularly important that the agencies involved should have been in consultation with each other before the referral. Such units may accept a child or family for treatment if this is considered appropriate and if the child protection and legal issues are resolved. It is important that the current carer acknowledges that abuse has taken place and wants psychological help for the child or help over parenting issues. These units as such have no statutory responsibilities regarding child sexual abuse, although some social services staff within them might. They sometimes contribute to the formal assessment of a child's educational needs. All residential and day units have their own school component for children who require help for some time.

The Cleveland Report[6] emphasised the importance of multi-professional involvement in the identification of and work with sexually abused children. Nobody should try to deal with such a situation on their own. The Department of Education and Science issued all education authorities with a circular[7] setting out recommended procedures for teachers to follow in the case of actual or suspected abuse. Schools must alert the statutory agencies in such cases and local education authorities have circulated information to their schools on how to deal with this. All schools are recommended to designate a senior member of staff as co-ordinator to ensure that the authority's procedures are followed and to liaise with other agencies. These teachers are the pivotal point in the care of sexually abused children within the school.

Confidentiality

The question of confidentiality within a school is complex. The school will probably be represented at relevant case conferences and it is the head teacher's responsibility to ensure that members of staff most directly involved with a child at risk are aware of the current situation and are particularly observant. This information must be regarded by those concerned as strictly confidential. When a child moves school and records are sent on, confidential records are kept under separate cover.

The situation regarding a sexually abused child who is no longer 'at risk' of abuse is less clear. If a child's circumstances affect performance in school then all teachers in contact need to be aware of these difficulties so that they can help make the most of the child's academic potential, or at least have realistic expectations of the child. In some cases it is important that relevant teachers know about the nature of the abuse so that they can understand and work with the child's behaviour. In other situations, it is more appropriate for teachers to know that the child is one who has been or is experiencing stress rather than details of the abuse.

Sometimes a child disclosing abuse for the first time to a teacher will ask for the information to go no further and the teacher, while attempting to retain the child's trust, must explain that he or she must pass it on. Teachers may also be required to support children who feel that they are being stigmatised.

Parents may well request confidentiality, at least of those attending case conferences. Decisions regarding confidentiality must be based on the best interests of the child where they do not conflict with the requirements of the law. Making such decisions will inevitably test existing relationships between the school and the child and family, and between the school and the other professionals involved.

The need for training

The sexual abuse of children challenges the norms of all societies and arouses a variety of emotions in us all. Teachers, like all professionals, must explore their attitudes and values and must investigate and understand their own feelings about the nature of sexuality before working with these children. Training is therefore of great importance both during initial teacher training and in later in-service teaching. The teacher, unlike other adults in the child's life, has to interact appropriately with the child in a setting of other children, imparting knowledge and maintaining respect. A formidable task, indeed, which will be recognised as such particularly by residential care workers and experienced foster carers. Definitions and checklists of signs of abuse must be critically examined and listening and responding skills developed if a child-centred approach to this area of work is to be adopted in school. Unfortunately, in spite of the guidelines, the Department of Education and Science has to date made no provision to authorities for child protection training.

Some teachers involved in a child's initial disclosure of abuse complain that their authority's guidelines, either directly or indirectly, instruct them to hand matters over to social workers or the police, thereby giving up any further involvement. This is virtually impossible by the very nature of the teacher's position. Of course social workers and the police must be involved and have a statutory duty to be so, but teachers also remain involved and training must prepare them for this. The response to abused children in the classroom may be crucial to their future welfare and development. The powerlessness felt by a teacher who is marginalised can result in considerable anger and frustration, especially when the decisions of others may seem inappropriate. Teachers are well placed to observe children, to monitor changes, to listen and even counsel if abuse is acknowledged, and training materials are increasingly being developed which recognise these roles.[8, 9] Teachers, however, are not trained for the primary guidance of sexually abused children.

Conclusion

Children in the classroom today are the adults of tomorrow. They have little or no political recognition as individuals but are often seen as the property of their parents. The Children Act 1989 attempts to redress this balance, recognising in its provisions that, until children are seen as 'equals', as people with appropriate personal rights and freedoms, we fail to protect them adequately from suffering inflicted by adults. The school is a microcosm of the community at large. The presence of respected adults of both genders and of different races and cultures, who treat children with respect and in an age-appropriate manner, can serve to empower them. In such an atmosphere, for example, black children will be less afraid that they are feeding racism by talking about their abuse.

Education should aim to improve children's emotional and social adjustment by increasing their awareness and acceptance of the best ways in which feelings, attitudes and values influence interpersonal behaviour. This is a complex role for schools. It is not simply a matter of what to teach but also requires an analysis of, for example, the factors which contribute to an abusing environment and the way in which schools might affect these. Unfortunately, carers cannot expect this degree of awareness from all schools as training is lacking at present in this area. Carers do, however, have the right to expect schools to treat their children with respect and in an age-appropriate manner. Denigrating remarks are unacceptable. Carers should be kept informed of their child's progress and can expect the school to use the skills and mechanisms available to it in attempting to meet the educational needs of the child.

Teachers have an important role to play in cases of child abuse. They can help in the detection and reporting of abuse; in working within a multi-agency teamwork environment; in contributing to the continuing support and monitoring of abused children; and in preparing children to cope with potentially abusing environments. However, it is only when the school has established how it will work, when all the teachers in the school are alert to the problems of abuse and how they should act, when the expertise of individual teachers has been identified and a proper inter-professional network has been set up (for example a school-based team of teacher, nurse, doctor and educational psychologist), that schools can fulfil their potential regarding child safety and development. In my experience, teachers are motivated to tackle these issues and to create an atmosphere in school that will foster the children's self-esteem and offer some power to them in their own lives.

References

1   Doyle C 'Sex abuse: Giving help to the children: A practical guide for concerned professionals' *Children and society* 1 3, 1987.

2   Bedford A *Child abuse and risk* Occasional papers series No 2, NSPCC, 1987.

3   Warnock H A *Special educational needs: report of the committee of enquiry into the education of handicapped children and young people* HMSO, 1978.

4   Adams W 'Working together to improve the supportive framework for children with special needs in mainstream schools: a multi-professional approach' *Maladjustment and therapeutic education* 6 no 2, 1988.

5   Children Act 1989, Section 36.

6   Butler-Sloss E *Report of the inquiry into child abuse in Cleveland* HMSO, 1987.

7   *Working together for the protection of children from abuse: procedures within the education services* DES 4/1988.

8   Braun D *Responding to child abuse – action and planning for teachers and other professionals* Bedford Square Press,1988 (reprint 1990).

9   Peake A *Working with sexually abused children: a resource for professionals* (practice papers and children's material) Children's Society, 1990 (new edition).

Bibliography

Mahony P 'Who pays the price? Sex abuse and education' *Gender and education* 1 1, 1989.

Milner J and Blyth E *Coping with child sexual abuse – a guide for teachers* Longmans, 1989.

Webster B 'Child sexual abuse prevention: a new role for teachers' *Links* 14 1, 1988.

6 Child sexual abuse and assessment of substitute families

Pat Francis

Pat Francis is project leader at Barnardo's New Families in Humberside. Some years ago she and her colleagues were forced by circumstances to face the possibility that carers could be abusers. In this chapter she describes how the team worked through this crisis and devised an assessment process through which applicants could be helped to examine their own feelings about sexual abuse. She calls for awareness of the need to develop expertise and knowledge in this area.

Introduction

The recognition of the prevalence and magnitude of child sexual abuse in Britain today is still relatively new. It is a highly-charged and emotional topic about which everyone has an opinion and very few answers. This paper attempts to address one of the most difficult areas of child care practice. How can we find 'safe' substitute families for vulnerable and hurt children who have been sexually abused?

This paper will examine the practical experience of one Barnardo's New Families Project in relation to child sexual abuse, some of the available research evidence, and our attempts to incorporate this evidence in a systematic way in our assessment work with adopters and foster carers.

Our practical experience

This Project, like many other adoption agencies throughout the country, now has a majority of children on referral who are known to have been sexually abused. These are children 18 months and upwards in age. An increasing proportion form part of large family groups of both boys and girls. The sexual abuse they have experienced is clear and horrific. The children describe buggery, oral sex with violence, sado-masochism, 'loving seduction' of four-year-olds and sexual abuse of their sons by mothers and grandmothers.

Like most professionals, we learned to cope to some extent with children's pain and distress by placing such activities outside our own personal frame of reference – people 'out there' do these sorts of things, but not our families, friends or acquaintances. Then some years ago we placed for adoption two sisters, six and eight years old, who had been fostered since babyhood. Many of us knew the foster carers and had placed other children in their home. The older child was seen as mentally handicapped with extreme behavioural problems associated with the disability. The other was a 'good' little girl who was able to express little genuine feeling.

After a short time in the adoptive placement, the eight-year-old began to give clear messages through drawings and verbal signals that she had been sexually abused. She eventually disclosed to her adoptive mother oral and anal intercourse, violence, tying-up and fantasy sexual 'games'. Her sister was only once able to disclose 'loving seduction'. This abuse they said was by their foster father with the knowledge of their foster mother. The older child, although intellectually limited, was not 'handicapped', but gave all the signs of mental illness through prolonged and systematic sexual abuse.

The effect on all Project members was dramatic. Suddenly our attempts to limit sexual abuse to 'unknown others' became impossible. Like many professionals involved with the family, we had not seen what was happening. If this family could do such things, who could be trusted? This could happen in our own families, with our friends, our babysitters. How could we ever dare to place a sexually abused child, or any child, into a family again? How could we tell which was a 'safe' substitute family and which was not?

Research

We searched the literature for information which could help us to be alert to individuals and families who were actual or potential sexual abusers. Virtually all that we could find were profiles of male perpetrators and sexually abusing families. We could find nothing on assessment of foster or adoptive applicants. The following is a brief summary of what was available and possibly relevant to our particular needs.

Profiles of perpetrators

Various research studies of perpetrators provided a wide range of characteristics – low self-esteem, poor self-image, negative view of women, sexually preoccupied, victims themselves, drink and drug abuse, violent or passive personalities. Finkelhor[1] stated that there is no single comprehensive profile of a perpetrator. Arguments ranged between those who opted for a psycho-pathology model[2] and those who perceived sexual abuse more in terms of misuse of power.[3] Meiselman's study[4] revealed that 80 per cent of fathers involved in incest had no hint of mental illness. He found the apparent 'normality' of these rather confusing.

Sexually abusing families

Furniss[5] suggested that sexually abusing families can be seen as falling into two categories: the so-called 'conflict-avoiding family' and the 'conflict-regulating family'.

Perhaps less well-known but equally helpful was Bedford's[6] presentation of the work of Holder and Mohr,[7] who contended that the following cluster of factors could clearly differentiate abusing from non-abusing families:

- the family seems to be moralistic and to avoid interaction with outsiders

- their apparent self-sufficiency is a consequence of their shyness, their feelings of inferiority and rigidity

- they are hopeless and anxious with feelings of sexual insufficiency

- there may be an interchange of mother and daughter roles

- communication within the family is minimal, secrets are maintained

- the mothers are often immature, passive and over-dependent, therefore providing little empathy or emotional support to the child victim.

The above provided some limited help in our task of assessing for 'safe' families. All Project social workers were given the above information to be used only as the broadest of guidelines in their assessment work.

The propositions from two researchers reinforced our anxiety and sense of responsibility in the work that needed to be done. Finkelhor[8] noted that step-daughters who live in step-families are 'universally vulnerable' and that children with disabilities or emotional problems are a high risk group. Garbino and Gilliam[9] noted that step-daughter/step-father relationships seem particularly risky, possibly because this combines the authority and opportunities for exploitation that parenthood brings 'without the natural inhibitions of consanguinity'.

Assessment: the social worker

The law requires social workers to assess the suitability of adoptive and foster carers. Interestingly, not even the Department of Health guidance handbooks directly address issues of child sexual abuse. Clearly this issue had to be addressed; the question for us was 'how?'.

Our own experience was that to view our professional work through appropriately-focused child sexual abuse spectacles, we ourselves had to go through a long personal adjustment. This could be likened to a grief cycle brought on by loss of innocence. The emotions were those of grieving, that is denial, guilt, blame, anger/rage, depression and finally some sort of acceptance/resolution. The danger for the children and families is when a worker becomes stuck in one phase of this 'bereavement' cycle. Most frequently it is at the point of denial.

Issues of sexuality are not commonly part of social work training. A course with a Relate[10] sex therapist assisted us enormously to become comfortable in the discussion of early sexual experience, attitudes to sexual growth and development and the quality of a family's past and present sex life. Ongoing training in child sexual abuse, together with play therapy sessions with sexually abused children, is an appropriate and constant reminder of the pain of the children and our need to be as thorough as we can in our assessment of new families. Too often, it seems, social workers who are preparing substitute families are removed from the raw pain and distress of the children, only reading sanitised versions in BAAF forms E and the like. First-hand experience of the children and their needs is crucial in proper preparation of adoption and foster carers.

The assessment process

Information giving
The fact that a majority of children on referral to the Project were known to have been sexually abused helped us in the early stages to

talk to prospective adopters about the need for 'safe' families. From practical experience we now know that many children will only disclose their abuse in the security of an adoptive family and so we stress the *likelihood* of such disclosures to all people thinking about adoption.

As part of the information-giving stage, which consists of an interview with a social worker and a full day's group meeting, our need to investigate and assess as to whether the applicants' family is a safe one is stated very clearly. Our reasons are twofold: first, we believe we must be open about what the procedures will entail, and second, we hope that this will make potential sexual abusers think twice before making an application to us. Only after the families have attended both information sessions can they make an application to adopt.

Information collection – are there good reasons not to proceed with this application?
This phase is basically about obtaining statutory and personal references, police checks, medicals etc, and is also used to obtain a broad picture of the family through the use of ecomaps* and geneograms.†

In relation to child sexual abuse the following have been included with the knowledge and permission of the applicants:

- all referees are asked specifically, in writing and verbally, whether they have any reason to believe that this person/family would physically or sexually abuse a child

- those applicants who have been married previously are asked to give their permission for us to contact either their ex-spouse or a referee who knew them well during the time of their previous marriage. Occasionally an adult child of the previous marriage is a satisfactory alternative. The only reason we contact these people is

---

* ecomap: a diagram, usually circles and continuous or dotted lines, to show the applicant's relationship with groups and organisations in the community
† geneogram: a diagram of relationships within a family

to ask whether they believe, on the basis of their past knowledge of the applicant, whether he/she would physically or sexually abuse a child.

In the two years we have used these specific procedures, we have never had an applicant refuse to allow us to contact such people, or make a complaint about the questions themselves. Despite some initial anxieties about the type of information we would receive from ex-spouses, particularly when the parting was acrimonious, we have always found these references to the point and useful. Once all the information has been collected and any obvious problem areas identified and shared with the family, a brief report is written for our adoption panel. This asks for the panel's recommendation to the agency as to whether this application should proceed or not. All applicants have the right to have such a presentation made. As with a full application for approval as adopters, the final decision is made by the agency.

This early presentation to the panel allows panel members the opportunity to raise areas for further investigation which they will want addressed in the final report. The adopters do not see this early report to the panel as it is basically 'third party' and therefore confidential information. They know that we may not be able to tell them why their application cannot proceed, although in fact this has never happened. We find that people relax considerably after their application has been to the first panel. This may be because they feel they are past the first 'hurdle', or because they know that subsequent judgements made by the social worker will be shared and discussed fully with them. Whatever the reason, we find this division of the procedures extremely useful.

Family and individual interviews – are there good reasons to recommend approval as adopters?
This phase of the assessment process is always the most professionally challenging and never more so than when child sexual abuse is in mind.

The family form A long family form is given to applicants to fill out to the best of their ability. This covers all the areas traditionally of interest to adoption social workers included in BAAF form F. We have added very specific questions for each applicant about how they learned the facts of life, previous significant relationships and whether there were any children, courtship and adjustments to sex, and finally questions about the present sexual relationship. The questions are all put simply and directly. Often sections are separated for both partners to complete. The following are examples of what is asked of each applicant:

FAMILY BACKGROUND
What was it like to be a teenager?
How did you find out about the facts of life?
Did you have girlfriends/boyfriends?

PREVIOUS RELATIONSHIPS
Did you have any previous significant relationships?
Could you tell us something about them and what happened?
Did you have any children?
How did you cope when the relationships ended?
What difficulties did you experience?
What present contact is there?

AND OF SINGLE APPLICANTS
Do you have a significant relationship with someone who does not live with you?
Is your relationship stable and satisfying, and if so why?
What are the areas of strain?
If you have a sexual relationship at present, is it satisfying to you? Can you say why?

Applicants take as long as they wish to fill these forms in and individual interviews begin on the basis of information within or left out of these forms.

Individual interviews Each applicant is asked, amongst other questions, whether they feel a child would be 'safe' in their family, and about issues of sexuality, growing up and so on. They are also asked if there are matters they wish to discuss which are not known to their partner. It is important here thinking through any 'secrets' carefully with the applicant.

Family interview By this time the family will have had the opportunity to talk together, put in writing and talk individually with the social worker about their opinions, experiences and thoughts relating to themselves and their family.

In relation to child sexual abuse, the social worker in particular will examine the following:

THE ADULTS' AND CHILDREN'S ABILITY TO BE OPEN AND COMFORTABLE ABOUT BODILY PARTS

We use simple blank gingerbread type figures and ask the family, individually, to put in their family names for the obvious male and female parts. Even young children have family language for these and the words used are often surprising and hilarious. The whole family will have previously participated in doing ecomaps and geneograms and will therefore be used to working with pens and paper.

The social worker will watch the non-verbal as well as the verbal communication, who children choose to help, how each participant handles the exercise, and so on.

The next stage is for the family to write down unacceptable as well as acceptable words for the bodily parts. Often children know words which are unacceptable and the sharing of these enables discussion of what a 'new' child may say and how these words may be handled by the whole family. The social worker will look for openness, tolerance, boundaries and understanding from the family in this exercise. This also enables the parents either to start or to continue to discuss sexual acting-out by the new child which may involve children of the family.

POWER RELATIONSHIPS WITHIN THE FAMILY

There are many opportunities to observe or to hear how power issues are dealt with in the family, or to enable the family to recognise these. They come from situations or stories of past incidents as well as from discussion about the adults' sexual adjustment over time. The ability of each to say 'no' to the other in all sorts of circumstances can be a simple indicator.

FAMILY BOUNDARIES

What is done, shown to, or discussed with children is obviously of significance to those who have been sexually abused, but also relevant to keeping a child safe. Discussions will revolve around nudity, who baths a child and whether this changes with age, whether a child comes for a cuddle in bed in the morning or sleeps every night with the parents, personal space, and so on. Every family will be different but notions about boundaries and why they are necessary are explored.

'OPEN' AND 'CLOSED' FAMILIES

Families who have no support networks, who are isolated and interdependent to an extreme, would raise workers' anxieties, not only in relation to child sexual abuse, but in terms of support for any new and demanding child.

A FAMILY'S ABILITY TO ACCEPT AND EXPRESS FEELINGS

More and more this is becoming a major focus in our assessment work, in recognition of the difficulty that some men in particular experience in talking about such things. Considerable time and effort is spent by Project workers to ensure, as far as possible, that feelings can be expressed and accepted within a family. In particular how families cope with anger and stress seems important with regard to sexual abuse.[11]

FAMILY SECRETS

These may emerge in individual interviews or may be shared by the adults and not the children. Within boundaries of commonsense, we talk with people about the danger of secrets and encourage sharing and openness. One example would be of a woman who disclosed to the project worker her own sexual abuse as a child. She, with help, decided to share this with her husband and later with her mother. She has made an excellent adoptive mother to a sexually abused boy.

ADULT UNDERSTANDING OF NORMS AND TABOOS

The possible temptations to a non-blood-related adult from a sexualised, or even a non-sexualised, child are discussed and examined. Strengths in this regard are particularly difficult to assess, but at least each adult applicant is made aware of the complexities and possible problems.

Panel approval All of the above issues are addressed in the final BAAF form F which is presented to the adoption panel. Our panel members have undertaken training in child sexual abuse and are very aware of their responsibility in the approval process. We find this shared responsibility invaluable.

Conclusion

This paper is intended to be read as a practice paper for those whose task it is to assess prospective adopters and foster carers. It is not a definitive statement on this work, only one agency's attempt to address what we believe to be hitherto unexamined areas of work.

The practice and thinking described has been done by a team of four highly experienced and capable social workers. The personal pain that has been felt in trying to come to grips with these challenging issues should not be underestimated. The fear that we may, despite all of our attempts to assess accurately, approve further abusing families is very real, and it does not go away. There are major issues here for agencies and managers in terms of support, training and, on occasions, personal counselling.

It seems clear that work must continue to develop expertise and knowledge in this area. Just to acknowledge the difficulty and view it as an impossible one to address is not good enough – for social work as a profession or for the children we have a duty to serve.

References

1   Finkelhor D *Child sexual abuse: new theory and research* Canada: Collier MacMillan Inc, 1979.

2   Gebhard P, Gagnon J, Pomeroy W and Christenson C *Sex offenders: an analysis of types* New York: Harper and Row, 1965.

3   Groth A N *Men who rape: the psychology of the offender* New York: Plenum, 1979.

4   Meiselman K C *Incest: a psychological study of the causes and effects with treatment recommendations* San Francisco: Jossey-Bass, 1978.

5   Furniss T 'Conflict-avoiding and conflict-regulating patterns in incest and child sexual abuse' *Acta Paedopsyschiatrica* 50 6, 1984.

6   Bedford A *Child abuse and risk* Occasional papers series No 2, NSPCC, 1987.

7   Holder W and Mohr C *Helping in child protective services* Tanglewood, Colorado: American Humane Association, 1980.

8   See 1 above.

9   Garbino J and Gilliam G *Understanding abusive families* New York: Lexington Books, 1980.

10 Relate (formerly Marriage Guidance Council) Central Office: Herbert Gray College, Little Church Street, Rugby CV21 3AP (telephone 0788 573241).

11 See 7 above.

7 An introductory training course for foster carers

Clare Devine and Ian Tate

Clare Devine is a teaching fellow on the child protection courses at the University of Dundee and was formerly senior social worker with the Royal Scottish Society for the Prevention of Cruelty to Children at the Overnewton Centre, Glasgow. Ian Tate is the Scottish officer of the National Foster Care Association. They describe in this chapter how they set about producing a course of training for foster carers who were already practising, and some of the issues which emerged. They emphasise throughout the importance of carers examining their own attitudes and feelings before embarking on the training of others.

Introduction

In 1988, like many local authorities, Strathclyde was becoming increasingly aware of the numbers of children in care who had been or were suspected of having been sexually abused. Children who had been received into care for other reasons were disclosing that they had been sexually abused prior to their period in care. There were also a few children who stated that they were being sexually abused in foster care. In order to acknowledge these developments, and in response to demands from foster carers themselves, a working group was established to develop training for foster carers which would be part of the region's child abuse training strategy. The authors of this paper were invited to join the working group and were delegated the task of designing and piloting the training.

The paper describes the process we engaged in to produce the training, its principles, aims, method and content and some of the issues which emerged.

The preparation process

This process raised questions about sexuality, gender and power. We decided that if foster carers were expected to face these issues then we had to do some preparatory work ourselves.

We began by looking at our own perspectives. Neither of us

80

could claim to be experts in work with sexually abused children, but jointly we had long experience of child care, an understanding of distressed and damaged children and their needs, and the stress and responsibility involved in providing consistent care for them. We agreed that our starting point would be an acknowledgement that sexually abused children are first and foremost children, with their own individual needs. This would be a crucial message for foster carers.

Then we looked at the facts. Research[1] told us that in the majority of cases children are sexually abused by a trusted male, who is known to them and who has responsibility for their care, either as a relative or friend. Children of both sexes are abused, though more girls are known to be abused than boys. Most abuse begins before puberty and some children are abused when very young. Considerable secrecy is associated with sexual abuse and children are subjected to threats to ensure the secret is kept. Children rarely lie but can quickly retract in order to keep the family secret or if they feel they are not believed. Emotional damage can continue into adulthood and can be long lasting. Perpetrators usually deny the abuse. Sexual abuse is not confined to a particular class or culture and is widespread. It is carried out in families by men who may appear responsible and respectable to the outside world.

Definitions of child sexual abuse[2] implied the abuse of power by a trusted adult (usually a male) over a dependent child. The abuse of power, the betrayal of trust, the denial of responsibility and the inability of children to consent appeared to be important themes in child sexual abuse. In practice, our impression was that children were not believed. Mothers were often blamed, held responsible for the abuse, and accused of collusion with the perpetrators. Men were believed and their denial colluded with.

We formulated a working hypothesis that the perpetrator was always responsible for his behaviour and must be controlled. Children needed to be believed and not blamed. By understanding the position of mothers and what it meant for them to accept that the man they trust has abused their child, their response, in most cases, could be considered as ambivalence rather than collusion. A mother's ambivalence had to be understood and worked with so that an alliance could be formed with her, to help her help her child.

Our training had to clarify this and its implications in foster care. Any intervention had to be based on principles of openness, honesty, consistency, trustworthiness, responsibility and the proper use of power. Workers needed to exercise power explicitly and non-abusively. We needed to be clear about relationships, boundaries and sexual behaviour. When working with sexually abused children, foster carers had to be careful not to damage a child's trust, not to collude with secrets and not to abuse their power. We agreed that training also had to address themes of power, gender, role and sexual behaviour.

This preparation, involving personal exploration, was a considerable learning experience for us, both as individuals and as collaborators, and one which we would recommend to trainers.

Aims of the course

It was decided that the course would be aimed at all foster carers. In some cases it is only when children feel safe in substitute care that they are able to tell about their abuse, so all foster carers should be informed regarding the needs of sexually abused children.

The aim of the course therefore was to create an awareness and understanding of child sexual abuse and to offer foster carers the opportunity to clarify and identify their own values and attitudes in relation to sexual abuse, sexuality, gender and power relations. More specifically, by the end of the course it was hoped that carers and workers would have developed an understanding of the needs of the sexually abused child, of the non-abusing parent, and of the perpetrator. It was intended also that participants would have a better understanding of the role of carers and other workers, particularly social workers, and would feel more confident about carrying out their own role.

Methods

The course was based on principles of adult learning, acknowledging that carers would bring with them their own experiences, knowledge and skills, particularly about caring for children, to be harnessed and developed. The training would emphasise that sexually abused children are children and that foster carers know about children.

Brainstorming, role play, audio and video material and some input by tutors would be the range of methods used. In order to offer foster carers an opportunity to build a trusting and learning environment small task groups would retain the same membership throughout. Discussion and dialogue would be key features. Handouts were provided as source material and for reference after the course. Our role as trainers was to provide the structure and create an environment to facilitate learning and to 'hold' feelings so that they could be faced and worked through. The course was run as a three-day block. Thirteen foster mothers and three social workers (one woman and two men) participated.

Course outline

The first day offered an opportunity to carers to identify their fears, concerns and uncertainties about child sexual abuse. This was done in a brainstorming exercise which gave everyone a chance to participate. Definitions and examples of child sexual abuse were considered, and facts and figures were used to demonstrate the reality of abuse. Links were made to practice. The need was acknowledged for foster carers and other workers to take responsibility for their own actions, to consider the wishes and feelings of the child and not to abuse their own power.

To demonstrate the reality of abuse, facts and figures of child sexual abuse were considered. Participants were asked to reflect on why they thought adults – mainly men – abuse children. Ideas and attitudes began to emerge as did the themes of betrayal of trust, abuse of power, denial of responsibility, the child's inability to consent, and the different expectations of men and women with regard to responsibility for sexual behaviour. All of the day's content was reflected upon in the day's final session in the large group.

The second day focused on ways to help the child, especially regarding telling about abuse. Verbal and non-verbal communication, particularly about sex and sexual behaviour, was considered from the child's perspective.

It was important to link with the previous day, noting issues, themes and feelings which were still around. The morning consisted of two exercises, one about verbal communication, the other about physical communication. The first exercise aimed at freeing the participants to put into words the kind of language a child might use to describe sexual activity, recognising that this may or may not be the language of the foster carers. It was important for the trainers to set the right tone during this exercise. There was much embarrassed laughter and it seemed important to give people space to express their embarrassment and discomfort about using what they saw as 'dirty' language. It was also important to recognise that not everyone knew the meaning of all of the words and that it was important to ask children, in a matter of fact way, to explain what they meant and, if appropriate, to provide them with the 'proper' word. As trainers, we had to demonstrate our own ability to deal with this kind of language in an unembarrassed fashion and, at the same time, not to get drawn into using it inappropriately.

The second exercise looked at 'good touch – bad touch'. There were obvious examples of 'bad touch' on which everyone agreed, but there were also grey areas which indicated different attitudes about physical contact. Participants were helped to understand how sexually abused children, because of their experiences, may misinterpret what a carer may consider as 'ordinary' physical contact. This can be a sensitive issue for male carers. It was important to stress the need for adults to take responsibility for their own behaviour. For example, it is not the foster mother's task to 'police' the child and foster father, nor to 'protect' him from the child. There needs to be open communication between everyone involved with the child about what is acceptable touch and behaviour. Carers are required to give children clear messages about this and to offer non-sexualised ways of showing affection.

NFCA's video[3] of foster mothers talking about their experiences of caring for sexually abused children highlighted some of the issues already identified and thus reassured participants. It also identified other issues still to be covered, so setting a new agenda.

The afternoon session concentrated on role play of a child attempting to tell about her abuse. This was a powerful and moving learning experience, getting in touch with the child's feelings and perspective. This exercise led to carers reflecting on personal experiences of listening (or not listening) to children in their care.

The final morning focused on the non-abusing parent. Participants explored the dilemmas that mothers have to face in accepting that their child has been abused by a partner or other trusted male carer. The ability to identify with the non-abusing parent was explored. This led to recognition of the importance of the mother to the child and of the need for her to be involved whenever possible.

This in turn led to the perpetrators, and to issues of male sexual behaviour. Strong feelings were expressed, some rooted in personal experience. The trainers had to hold these feelings and to facilitate thinking about the child's perception of the perpetrator. The need to enable abusers to acknowledge and change their behaviour was considered, while emphasising that this was not the foster carer's task.

The afternoon session aimed at placing child sexual abuse back into the broader child care context, recognising the need for parents to be part of the child care and protection team. This 'normalisation' process aimed at leaving foster carers confident and competent in their professional role.

A final evaluation session looked back to the issues identified in the brainstorming of the first day and checked out what had been covered and what had been missed out. Participants found that most topics had been covered at a depth which they had not expected. It was recognised that learning is a continuing process, through practice, through other training opportunities and most important through good support and supervision. The message was received that foster carers should not be left to care for children in isolation and that carers should be confident in demanding support, co-operation and resources from social workers and their agency.

In evaluation, all participants found the course a powerful and emotive three days. The following is a typical comment: 'I thoroughly enjoyed the course and was made to feel as though anything I said was important. Some parts of the course were light-hearted as well which helped relax us with one another and so it was easier to talk. I feel very confident now and hope I can give any sexually abused children that I foster both the comfort and understanding they need.' All thought they had gained a better understanding of child sexual abuse with some wanting the opportunity for further exploration. They also felt that they had a better understanding of the children, their mothers and the perpetrators. Some carers who already fostered sexually abused children discovered that they had dealt with them sensitively and well; a measure of this was the child's disclosure to them about previous abuse. Other carers thought they were more prepared to care for a child in the future. One or two said that, if they had realised what it entailed, they would have been afraid to continue their application to foster. However, given the confidence derived from this experience, they felt able to face the responsibility of the task. One or two thought that, in the light of what they had learned, they would find it too difficult and stressful for them and their families to cope with a sexually abused child.

The issues

Child sexual abuse training is more than considering the facts, the causes, the prevalence and the incidence. Trainers have to address the feelings aroused in training as well as any theoretical understanding. We suggest that if the feeling content is not faced and made sense of, other learning will be blocked. Time has to be included for discussion and reflection during any training course.

Trainers need to be comfortable enough in working together with feelings and group dynamics. We realised that our own preparation process was crucial in enabling us to do this. We also found it useful to demonstrate working together as male and female trainers.

Participants may well have experienced abuse themselves and training may give rise to a need to talk about these experiences. We acknowledged this often during the introduction to the course and established some ground rules about respect for each other's contribution, confidentiality and the responsibility we all had for learning. It was important to establish that this was not a therapeutic group, although some people might want to draw on their own experiences as part of their own learning process. It was made clear that trainers would be available for individual consultation at coffee breaks and over lunch. The majority of participants (all foster mothers) said that they had experiences which they felt had been abusive. One can only speculate on what might emerge in a group with a more even gender balance. Trainers should be aware of this dimension of training and create a climate in which it can be faced.

Practice issues also emerged. A major one was how carers should deal with a child's disclosure. Not offering a child false promises about keeping the secret was discussed. It was also made clear that information forthcoming about a child who might be at risk could not remain confidential to the group. Trainers, with the individual concerned, must decide the most helpful way of passing the information to the appropriate agency. It was agreed that foster carers should be closely involved in investigative and further disclosure work. Foster carers can be excluded and isolated from the child as the 'experts' take over, for instance when the child is receiving specialist help. The foster carer's task may then be seen as escort for the child rather than as a key member of the team with a particular knowledge of and relationship with the child.

Foster carers are in a unique position to pick up clues about abuse from a child's behaviour or conversation. They need the opportunity to discuss their observations in order to make sense of them and, if appropriate, to help the child to disclose. Too often, it seems, social workers reassure, rationalise or ignore foster carers' sometimes tentative requests for help for children.

Another source of concern for carers is sexualised behaviour. They need the opportunity to discuss how best to manage it. In discussing this sensitive area foster carers were not seeking blanket rules, rather they wanted to reflect on ways of helping children in the context of the foster family, with its own standards and norms.

Contact with birth parents was a frequent issue. Carers could see the need for the child to have contact with the mother but were more ambivalent about contact with the perpetrator. Some had had experiences of perpetrators visiting their homes which had left them feeling vulnerable. It was felt that this kind of contact should not be left to carers to manage and control and that it was not always appropriate for it to take place in what children now perceived as their 'safe' territory. Again it was thought that social workers must take responsibility for organising, managing and supervising contact.

Carers felt that sometimes they were abused by the system. Decisions, they felt, were made elsewhere, very often by people in power whom they felt did not know them or the child they were caring for. On the whole, individual social workers tried to be helpful but, like the carers, seemed powerless, unsupported and at times deskilled by the system.

Listening to the carers over three days, we were struck by the level of commitment to the children in their care and to fostering in general. Their skill in communicating with children on a variety of levels and their ability to provide safe caring environments was evident in their talk about the children they had cared for.

A three-day training course can only begin to address the feelings, issues and dilemmas involved in the care of abused children. At the end of the course it was clear that foster carers require honest and realistic preparation for the job, yet all the preparation in the world could not make the reality of caring for a particular child less worrying, painful or disturbing. To care for a child well, in addition to their knowledge and insight carers require practical and emotional support as part of a child care team.

References

1 La Fontaine J S 'Child sexual abuse' Research Briefing ESRC, 1988.

2 Schecter, Roberge and SCOSAC in Glaser D and Frosj S *Child sexual abuse* Macmillan, 1988.

3 'Caring for sexually abused children: conversations with foster carers' video, NFCA 1987.

8 Fostering young people who have been sexually abused

Edna Davis, Barbara McKay, Loura McStae,
Keith Pringle and Shelagh Scott

The authors of this chapter are social workers for the Family Placement Project, Barnardo's North East Division. Early in 1988 they set up a crisis and assessment placement service offering assessment in foster care for young people who had been sexually abused. They discuss here the support provided for their carers, both individually and in peer groups, and identify nine main issues for consideration that have arisen from this project.

Introduction

The Family Placement Project (FPP) of Barnardo's North East Division is a well-established resource offering time-limited, task-centred foster care placements ranging from six months to four years to teenagers in local authority care. We use specialist, professional foster carers who are fee-paid in recognition of the nature and difficulty of their task. Due to increasing awareness about child sexual abuse and growing appreciation of the potential therapeutic role of foster carers, the project trained all its foster families to help victims of sexual abuse in the period from autumn 1986 to spring 1988. We used a training programme specially designed for the task by three of the team's social workers, a programme later published by Barnardo's which has been incorporated into courses by a wide range of other agencies in Britain and overseas.[1] *All* existing foster carers in the project were trained, not only because the levels of known and suspected sexual abuse among referred children was very high, but also because we realised that any young person might have been abused in the past, regardless of whether this was suspected.

From the spring of 1988 the project also began to develop a radically new resource: a Crisis and Assessment Placement Service (CAPS) offering assessment in foster placement to sexually abused young people either at the point of disclosure or soon after. Each placement was planned to continue for no longer than six months and to focus on (i) assessing the needs of the young person in the long term, and (ii) providing first-rate therapeutic assistance to the young people from the foster carers if the young person wanted this. A pilot programme was started and the CAPS scheme at the time of writing has three fostering units in existence and one under assessment. It was envisaged that there would be little opportunity for matching in CAPS placements, so training and assessment of CAPS foster carers was especially comprehensive. It comprised 12 training/assessment group sessions using the Open University course 'Caring for children and young people' and the Project's own child sexual abuse (CSA) training programme, two videoed family groupwork sessions, and eight to 12 home assessment visits by a project worker. The CAPS scheme has now catered for a number of young people and we view it as a highly important new resource for teenagers. CAPS foster carers are also fee-paid at a higher rate!

This paper draws mainly on our experiences with the CAPS scheme but also uses material from the project's more established family placement service (which we refer to as our 'mainstream' scheme). We shall outline the framework within which we offer support to CAPS family placement units and then go on to discuss several issues which have proved especially difficult for some foster carers working in this field and which require careful attention from support workers. However, before discussing both the framework and the issues, it is important to stress that post-placement foster care support cannot be separated from the groundwork already achieved in the assessment and initial training phases. If the correct content and ethos has not been achieved at these earlier stages it is difficult to provide an effective support service. This will be apparent at several points in the analysis which follows.

Framework of post-placement support

During placements, CAPS foster carers would expect to receive regular weekly or fortnightly visits by their project support worker, who is also one of the staff who trained and assessed them. At times of crisis, which can be very often, visits would be far more frequent. Likewise a high level of input is expected from the young person's local authority social worker. The contribution of both social workers are regulated and defined as part of a formal placement agreement drawn up near the start of the placement. Such high level expectations of support from social workers reflects the demands placed on foster carers by the crisis and assessment elements of their task, a recognition of the emotionally draining potential of working with sexual abuse, and knowledge derived from recent research on fostering breakdowns.

The placement agreement also defines the system by which good communications are to be maintained both between the professionals (including the foster carers) *and* the young person and their natural family. If good liaison does not exist between all services involved then the main loser will be the young person – but another loser will be the carer. So the placement agreement not only stipulates regular (weekly or fortnightly) meetings between the core team of professionals and timing of reviews but also carefully lays down the role of the professionals. The foster carer, probably more than anyone else except the young person, benefits from knowing clearly who does what. Confusion and mixed messages lead only to frustration, a draining anger, and de-skilling. Educating other professionals to regard CAPS foster carers as colleagues and not semi-clients is of course a continuing task, not only for the project but to the foster carers themselves. The nature of the training they received emphasised that this educational process was part of their job. Their professional conduct in assessments and case conferences has vindicated this emphasis in their training and they are steadily winning professional status by their own practice.

Another vital part of the support process in the CAPS scheme is the fortnightly carer support group. In our experience this group is more supportive, at a deeper emotional level, than the many other support groups we have known. There are probably several reasons for this: in-depth working with a subject like sexual abuse can bring workers together in a powerful way; our original training material on CSA placed emphasis on sharing of emotional resources as much as on disseminating information; the very personal level at which the Open University training course operates; the personalities involved. Clearly this is an example of the way the original training and assessment model feeds into the post-placement support system.

The CAPS support group is primarily for support: on-going training is an important but secondary function. Although the group is facilitated by project workers, increasingly it is not led by them. Mutual support in the group consists not simply of practical advice from one group member to another but also genuine sharing of feelings. It seems to us that foster carers of sexually abused children must function at that deeply emotional level if the group is to be of maximum benefit: as anyone who has worked in the field of sexual abuse knows, it arouses deeply painful and personal emotions in those who want to be of more than superficial therapeutic value.

Moreover, many young people offload on to foster carers emotional material of the most highly charged nature. The question remains: where do foster carers offload this material if they are not to be overwhelmed? Weekly visits by a social worker are certainly not enough. Discussion with friends is ruled out by virtue of confidentiality. Some relief may be found in close relatives living in the household, for instance partners and adult children of the foster family, but this can often be too claustrophobic, and is of limited value to single female foster carers. Hence the value of using fellow foster carers.

Sharing difficulties in the CAPS support group often extends well beyond the group meetings. If one foster carer has a particular problem or is very weighed down by the mass of emotional material, he or she often contacts other foster carers directly for support. On a reciprocal basis, this is an effective means of support.

One issue which this chapter does not address is who cares for the carer's carers – that is how much and what type of support do the agency project workers receive to help them relieve the foster carers? This is a major question facing all agencies working in this field and requires an urgent answer, but it would need another chapter to do it justice. Instead, we turn now to consider nine issues which can cause major difficulty for foster carers working with sexual abuse. Each issue has relevance to other forms of foster care but is particularly problematic in this field.

Issues for foster carers

The need for respite
We have already noted the emotionally draining quality of sexual abuse work, and we discuss issues causing further strains below. Consequently it is essential that foster carers of abused young people are not expected to go on endlessly without respite. 'Mainstream' foster carers should have a right to respite care for the young people placed with them, and in the case of shorter term care, such as our CAPS scheme, it is essential that foster carers are allowed to have

breaks between placements. This may be difficult without a system of financial retainers, particularly for single people.

Dealing with problem behaviour

This work also requires extra stamina to deal with frequently severe behavioural problems; for all these young people will be carrying massive internal charges of anger, guilt, sadness, confusion and fear. Each will have different ways of expressing or dealing with these emotions, many of which will be extreme, including total withdrawal. Coping with such behaviour over months or sometimes years requires not only ingenuity but also energy. Hence there is the need for expert advice on practical behaviour management and space for foster carers to express their own rage, frustration and depression.

An opportunity for foster carers to remember their own needs

This again is especially a problem when foster carers are working with sexually abused young people. To do this work realistically requires someone with extremely high motivation, but occasionally this motivation itself can cause difficulties. If the essence of professionalism is an ability to maintain the primacy of the young person's needs, then the foster carers' high motivation can lead them to forget that sometimes their own needs have to be met before they will be able to fulfil their professional role physically and emotionally. The emotional pull of working with sexual abuse and the resonances which it sets up within carers occasionally leads to an overstretching of their own resources. For instance, it may be that a couple who are fostering put all their energies into meeting the overwhelming needs of the young person placed and forget to make room for their own relationship – and for their own individual space. This can lead to frustration, resentment and jealousy which might eventually jeopardise the placement, and defeat the object of the exercise. The support worker must continue to remind foster carers that they must look after themselves if they are going to be able to give the young person prime care, and must challenge them appropriately if this is not happening.

Recognising the potential impact on the dynamics of the foster family unit of working with sexual abuse

This is of particular concern where the fostering unit is a couple. The problem can take several forms. Given this project's views on causation of sexual abuse,[2] and the known preponderance of males as perpetrators, in most of our fostering units the woman is likely to do most of the direct therapeutic work with the young person, even if he is male. In most cases the role of the male carer is to share practical tasks and to act as the partner's main source of support, occasionally joining in with the direct emotional work *alongside* the female carer. In these circumstances male foster carers can sometimes resent the closeness built up between the female carer and the young person, either vying for their partner's attention or wanting to play a greater part with the young person than he or she is ready to countenance. Initial training and assessment should minimise such occurrences, but support workers need to be ready to spot such trends as early as possible and challenge them in a caring and therapeutic manner.

Again, some abused young people will confuse sexual contact with affection or due to their experiences will gravitate towards the male carer. This can be as true of young men as of young women. In such situations the male carer may, consciously or unconsciously, respond to such behaviour emotionally and/or sexually. Once again, initial training and assessment should have forewarned foster carers of this possibility, but this is no guarantee that such episodes will be avoided. The support worker needs to be ready to help foster carers halt such trends at an early stage by being honest about what they perceive to be happening and also perhaps by using family groupwork techniques, to readjust the balance in relationships between the young person and the two foster carers.

*Recognising the needs of the foster carer's own children**

There is always a danger in assessment, training and support that attention focuses on the foster carers exclusively to the detriment of natural children, including adults, who are living in the family home, or closely attached to it if living away. When working with sexual abuse, the lifestyle of the family may have to be substantially adjusted to meet the needs of the young person placed – and where that young person's previous sibling relationships may well have been

---

* A recent video *Children who foster*, produced by the Natural Children's Support Group, Foldyard House, Naburn, York YO1 4RU offers invaluable insights into this.

problematical. On both counts, foster carers and their support workers should prepare and consult natural children carefully, according to their age. Once more the process should begin at the assessment and training stage, but it has to continue. If even one person in the household, or vital to the household, comes to see the placement as not viable for them, then there is a serious risk of breakdown. Where such trends are noted after placement, use of family groupwork techniques may again be valuable.

Even if family groupwork per se is not utilised, that is involving the whole family in formally convened live supervised and/or videoed sessions, then many action techniques drawn from family therapy can be helpful in work with individuals, pairs, or indeed the whole family in a less formal framework. Such techniques could be role-playing, sculpting and doubling.

Extra professional stresses in working with sexual abuse
Extra professional stresses derive from the role of foster carers at child abuse case conferences and reviews; being the recipient of sexual abuse disclosures; accompanying young people to medical examinations; acting as a liaison between the young person and their birth family, whether or not the abuser is included; appearing as witnesses in court for care and possibly criminal proceedings. Stress derives from two sources in these circumstances: the actual performance of the role themselves; and also helping the young person with the strong flux of feelings such situations produce. As always, these areas should have been thoroughly considered in the initial assessment and training, but the practical issues and emotional turmoil will still cause problems each time they are encountered. Support workers must be ready to give advice on the practicalities as well as being there to receive the foster carer's feelings, just as the foster carer will be there to receive the feelings of the young person.

Accusations of sexual abuse from young people against foster carers
This is an issue which causes great distress not only when it occurs, but also when even the possibility of it is discussed with foster carers. Moreover, recently considerable emphasis has been placed on the threat to foster carers of false allegations by young people and others. We attempt to consider this possibility realistically.

The vast majority of research[3] confirms that it is extremely rare for young people deliberately to make false allegations of sexual abuse against anyone. Consequently our message as support workers to foster carers is that it is highly unlikely that they will be accused unless a) they do abuse the young person, or b) their behaviour is misinterpreted by the young person. So in the initial training and in post-placement support we advise on how to avoid both these occurrences. As regards the prevention of actual abuse, we point out to male foster carers that all men have some potential to abuse, though this varies according to life experiences, and that they should constantly monitor their own behaviour. To avoid actions which can be misinterpreted by young people we initially provide guidelines to foster carers which we regularly reinforce. We ask them to bear in mind the precise circumstances in which the young people were originally abused; these will be danger areas for the young person in terms of daily living – for instance, were they originally abused at bath-times, in the bedroom, when the female parent was absent from the home? In this way foster carers can avoid situations which seem innocuous to them but which may be fraught with sinister meaning for the young person. Provided that foster carers exercise caution in such situations and also do not actually abuse the young person, risks of accusation to the foster family from the teenager are virtually non-existent. Finally, we do not shrink from emphasising to foster families that there are cases frequently reported in the media where foster carers and social workers sexually abuse the vulnerable young people in their care. These facts are too serious not to face squarely.

Loss

Being close to, and engaging at a deep level with, young people who have undergone sexual trauma can quickly produce an unusually close bond between foster carer and teenager: the inevitable dissolution of this bond in time-limited and short-term fostering may be a source of great pain for both parties. Support workers cannot, of course, and should not remove the pain completely – but they can help to keep it manageable. For instance, it is useful for the foster carer gently to remind the young person right from the start that the placement does have an end-point: this also reinforces the fact to the foster carer.

Ritualistic sexual abuse

This final issue may seem melodramatic but we are increasingly aware from the literature[4] and from two cases in our own experience that 'satanic' and other forms of ritualistic abuse can be a very disturbing element in working in this field. If a young person has been abused in the context of a ritualistic sex ring, the stresses on the foster carer due to the young person's feelings and the nature of the investigations can be immense. Stresses on the carer's support network can also be heavy – and it is vital that the agency provides space for workers to make the appropriate input, and for workers themselves to receive adequate support.

Conclusion

This paper has outlined ways of assisting carers with the stress of fostering sexually abused young people. What all of us working in this area need to remember, however, is the potential for positive change which is offered to these young people by foster care – if the stresses can be limited and managed. Fostering of this nature does require special capacities and special people: people who recognise that the price of helping is high – but that the results are worth it.

References

1   Davis E, Kidd L and Pringle K *Child sexual abuse training programme for foster parents with teenager placements* Barnardo's, 1987.

2   Davis E, Kidd L and Pringle K 'Parents in training' *Community Care* 17 March 1988.

3   Salter A C *Treatment of sex offenders and victims* Sage Publications, 1988.

4   Hopkins J 'Ritualistic abuse' *Social Work Today* 26 October 1989.

9 A foster carer's view

Marion Burch

Marion Burch is a foster carer of many years' experience who has looked after a number of abused children, both long and short term. She describes at first hand the implications for the caring family and the importance of careful planning and recording, of building a relationship with the child, and of working with visiting parents. She also emphasises the importance of appropriate training for carers.

Introduction

Caring for someone else's child invariably promotes a complexity of feelings, but caring for someone else's sexually abused child commits the carer to a multiplicity of responsibilities and emotional turmoils.

Carers may be prepared for and knowingly accept such a child into their home, or they may discover some time later that a child in the midst of the family has previously been abused. Too late then to consider the implications for each member of the family and to wish that they had a deeper understanding of the needs of the child.

Carers need skills to recognise the signs and symptoms and not to make assumptions but to listen, to observe and then to manage behaviour resulting from abuse. Knowledge, understanding and acceptance of their own sexuality and that of their partner are also required, with a recognition of the limitations and coping capabilities of each family member as well as a determination to lead as normal a life as possible in the given circumstances. The depth of feelings into which they may be plunged has to be experienced to be believed.

Children in care are special and have specific needs; sexually abused children are very special and have many more; they are vulnerable children who will develop into vulnerable adults unless they receive appropriate help. Admission to care is traumatic for all children irrespective of age. They experience feelings of fear, guilt and pain, even though for some there may be accompanying feelings of relief.

Implications for the caring family

It is not easy to discuss sexual matters with a social worker who may be a complete stranger. It cannot be easy for the social worker either, being unable to anticipate a carer's reaction to a case history without perhaps feeling ill at ease themselves, or lacking the expertise to offer expert guidance.

Hearing details of abuse can arouse feelings of shock, disgust, disbelief, fear, incredulity, anger, intense sadness and sometimes, if carers are honest, a kind of sexual excitement. Not least, self-doubts can also be felt about their ability to meet the many needs of this child. The intensity of these feelings can depend on the nature of the abuse: hearing about an isolated sexual assault by a stranger on a child may not have the same impact as hearing about abuse by a person trusted by the child for years; hearing that a child has gained knowledge about sex by witnessing sexual acts between adults may make carers feel sad at this child's lost innocence but may be easier to accept than knowing that a child has been involved in pornography for financial gain. There has to be a frank and open discussion between partners and an acknowledgement of the emotional battering such a child can have on the most stable and trusting partnership.

Listening to a child disclosing abuse and retelling sexual acts with the perpetrator may evoke intense anger. This can be misplaced: it may be difficult to respond appropriately to other children in the home when carers are full of intense feelings with no time or space to deal with them. This may cause problems too, at times, in the sexual relationship with their partner. Hearing of abuse may recall memories, long forgotten and now resurfacing, of sexual assault in their own childhood. Also, realisation that a child has sexual knowledge beyond their years can feel threatening and can raise questions about a carer's own attitude to sex.

So, a distressing and difficult aspect of caring for a sexually abused child can be the effect on the carer; profound and irrational feelings can arise about the trustworthiness of the male members of one's own family among the feelings of guilt and anger that follow.

Carers must acknowledge that they run the risk of an allegation of abuse being made against themselves,* so it is a wise precaution to

---

* The National Foster Care Association's useful leaflet *Child abuse: accusations against foster carers* spells out the issues and gives advice.

arrange for an unobtrusive 'chaperone' when one of the carers is absent from home, and to give careful consideration to the choice of baby-sitters. Carers must not be without support in such a task. It is essential therefore to build a trusting relationship with the child's agency before undertaking the care of a child.

Planning a placement with the social worker

When a social worker first requests a placement, little may be known about the child's general background and even less about day-to-day care, and there may be no reason to suspect sexual abuse. For example:

> Paul was three years old when placed in foster care. He was aggressive and his speech was poor. Nine months later he began to 'act out' his sexual abuse through play.

> Ann, aged five years, was with foster carers for 18 months because of her birth mother's mental illness. She was then placed for adoption and six months later she disclosed abuse which she had experienced when she was three.

> Rebecca was 15 when the request for care was made. She had been abused for five years, but seven more passed before she was able to disclose the facts.

Conversely, placements may be made either as a result of a child's disclosure of abuse or of serious suspicion that abuse is occurring; this information should be available to the carer including, perhaps, details of the abuse.

Much has been written by BAAF, NFCA and others about planning a foster placement, introducing a child to a family, easing the child into their new home and supporting child and family thereafter. It is to be hoped that a carer receiving any child, whether or not abuse is suspected, will have received preparatory training in techniques that are helpful for child and family at this sensitive time. Suffice it to say here that neither carer nor agency can afford to cut corners in planning the placement of a child who has experienced abuse, especially when this has been by someone loved and trusted. Extra sensitivity will be required especially, for instance, at bedtime, because a bedroom may have been a frightening place for a child.

It is imperative, first, for social worker and carer to be clear about their respective roles and, second, for them to monitor how, subsequently, they interact. For instance, the degree to which the foster carers are involved with the birth family will depend upon this allocation of roles. As the placement develops, the roles may adjust to new circumstances but it is essential for social workers and carers to discuss and agree on why and how such adjustments are made.

An outline of responsibilities embodied in these respective roles follows.

The social worker should:

- share with the foster carer the work done with the parents without betraying confidentiality

- keep the foster carer informed of any change in the home circumstances of the birth parents which could affect the child

- liaise between birth parents and the foster carer

- inform the carer of any change in the local authority plans such as an application for a care order

- offer support to the foster carer and discuss the progress or lack of progress of the placement

- draw up a placement contract between birth parents, foster carer and the local authority

- assist where necessary in transporting the child to and from home visits

- see that parents have travel tokens/warrants/cash to cover the cost of visits

- in co-operation with the carer, help the child to understand why he or she is in care, and about any future plans

- arrange for the foster carer and birth parents to attend reviews.

The foster carer should:

- discuss all aspects of the placement with the social worker, including arranging contact between parents and child, helping parents to demonstrate their commitment to their child and to understand their child's behaviour

- provide a parenting model when birth parents visit, answer questions honestly and inform them of changes in the child's routine

- accept other members of the extended family who may wish to visit

- in co-operation with the social worker, help the child understand why he or she is in care, and about any future plans

- be involved in reviews and case conferences and give evidence in court.

When the child is placed

The first few weeks or months of a placement is often referred to as 'the honeymoon period' but, even when children appear to be contented with the new situation, they may not be able to express their true feelings. As the placement progresses and the child becomes increasingly integrated into the new family, real feelings will begin to emerge. The child may start to complain of various aches and pains, and minor cuts and bruises may be magnified out of all proportion. These expressions of emotional pain, low self-esteem and feelings of 'badness' can escalate, and children sometimes cut themselves with anything that is sharp or break toys and possessions. The carer can help by assuring them that they are in no way to blame for what has happened, rather that the blame lies firmly with the adults involved.

The child's anger, both at being separated from their family and at the abuse itself, can be violent and very difficult to deal with, especially when directed at younger children or animals. Offering safer ways to vent feelings can give immediate help, but the child may need more than this in order to come to terms with what has happened and begin to heal emotionally. Often such a child's poor social skills isolate them from 'normal' children, who are quick to observe the differences between themselves and the abused child but cannot understand the reasons for this; they only see a child who has difficulty in getting dressed or managing a knife and fork, or who may still bed wet, or disturb the whole family at night with sleep walking and nightmares. An abused child is often misunderstood, disliked and avoided by other children, and carers need to be prepared for this and make allowances for the child's resulting frustration.

School
Angry feelings can spill over into school life, as abused children can find themselves lonely and friendless there as well as in the foster home.

School can be a miserable place for a child whose low self-esteem and anxiety may have earned the label 'slow learner'. There may be other physical problems too which are causing learning difficulties, such as poor hearing and eyesight: all these, added to the feelings of failure, can lead to disruptive behaviour.

It is not fair to expect children to cope with a new school immediately upon arrival in a new home. A 'cover story' is required for them to explain their sudden appearance in the classroom; otherwise they might innocently tell the whole story of the abuse, thus either attracting too much curiosity or isolating themselves still further from their peers.

Sexualised behaviour
Some children, especially if emotionally deprived, are so desperate for affection and attention that they seek it indiscriminately from anyone, including strangers, and their need for close physical contact can result in behaviour that appears to be sexually provocative. Sexualised behaviour has brought rewards for such children in the past and may be used again to attract the affection and attention they crave. They need to hear very clearly from the carer that they are liked *for themselves*.

A child may also initiate and participate in sexualised play with other children, using innocent situations for sexual games. For example, a blanket placed on the ground is seen as a 'bed' and the play-house or tent becomes a house for 'secret games', or toys are used in a sexualised way. Great self control on the part of the carer is called for to deal calmly with a child who is simulating the sexual act and to redirect the play. Firm but sensitive guidance is required on how to play with other children and, above all, it is important that any feelings of guilt and self blame the child already has are not compounded by an angry or shocked response from the carer.

Friends, relatives and visitors to the foster home need tactful guidance so that they do not give the wrong 'messages' to a child. Again a cover story may be required to protect confidentiality. Close

103

relatives like grandparents, who may know more about the child's circumstances, may need help to behave naturally with the child.

Building a relationship

An abused child can take months or even years to build up a trusting relationship with carers. A carer can feel that the child is 'play acting', that is responding as expected by the adult but without real emotion, and that it is impossible to reach the hidden depths of feeling. There are times when a child wears a blank look and has difficulty in remembering simple family rules, needing constant reminders. This is especially apparent when there is uncertainty about timing and implementation of future plans.

Food can become an issue in the placement. A child may over-eat and constantly demand food and drink for comfort (even perhaps stealing and hoarding it), or may refuse food. Perhaps, at home, food was withheld or given as a reward for sex; or perhaps the perpetrator may have been the one who provided the food. If the male carer is the family cook, such a child needs to know that it is safe to eat in the new family.

Distrust and a feeling that life is out of control can cause defiant and provocative behaviour. Unless it is skilfully handled every request by the carer, no matter how simple, can become an issue and develop into a confrontation. It may feel as though the carer's patience is being tested to its limit. Allowing children to make choices whenever possible and encouraging them to accept a small challenge, for instance a new activity, will help them develop a sense of self-worth through achievement. The passing of time and a consistent approach will assist in building a trusting relationship although feelings may be reactivated with different events or at different stages of a child's development. Sometimes the behaviour described escalates as the child begins to trust the new situation and feels ready to talk about the abuse.

Disclosure

Sex is a taboo subject in many families and it is not easy for some children to talk about it. A younger or inarticulate child's first indication that abuse has occurred may be by 'playing it out' with ordinary dolls, and the carer will need sensitively to offer opportunities for further disclosure without any hint of coercion. There may be outside pressure on a carer to encourage a child to talk, but this is unfair. The agenda for telling is the child's, not the carer's, social worker's or police officer's, and children will tell about abuse in their own time and in their own way, to a person of their own choice. It should not reflect on the carer if the chosen time is after the child has left the family.

We know that children rarely lie about abuse, therefore it is imperative that the carer's reaction is one of belief. It may be difficult for a carer to remain calm and controlled, to absorb what the child has said and to respond sensitively without expressing feelings of anger towards the perpetrator. But the child needs to hear first that they are believed, second that they are in no way to blame, and third that the responsibility is the adult's. Then the child can be congratulated on the courage required in speaking out.

When a child has disclosed abuse for the first time the various procedures must be explained honestly and reassurances given to the child that they will not have to manage any of this on their own. It is the carer's responsibility to write down everything the child has said exactly as it was spoken, including names for the genital areas, and to inform the social worker immediately. Accurate records may prevent the child having to repeat the story over and over again. Recording dates, times and events pertaining to the child is essential, particularly if legal proceedings are a possibility. The carer may be asked to write a report for the court and may be expected to give evidence.

The social worker will follow the local authority's child abuse procedures and the carer should be familiar with these because the child will need the support and comfort of the carer throughout. The medical examination is usually carried out by a doctor skilled in dealing with child abuse victims, but wherever a child is, whether hospital, police station or foster home, sharing these traumatic experiences with children not only helps them but also gives the carer an awareness and insight that can be invaluable later.

Parental contact
Accepting parents into one's home can be difficult. It isn't easy to give a welcoming smile and offer tea to a parent who is suspected of abuse or known to have abused their child. However, it is right for parents and child to see each other unless there is a legal direction to the contrary, or unless the child absolutely refuses contact. The quality of

parental contact is very important and it is the carer's responsibility to enable parents to demonstrate their motivation and commitment to their child in as comfortable an environment as possible.

Visits to the foster home are stressful for both parents and carers, and conversation can be difficult. Tension may be eased by involving the parents in the day-to-day care of their child. This often frees them from feeling that they must bring presents in order to be accepted. Some ways of doing this are for parents to:

– prepare a meal for their child, or give their baby a feed

– take the child to and from school or nursery

– make the bed/cot, or wash and iron clothes

– play with the child, help them to read and write

– bath the child and put them to bed

– choose clothes for the following day (this is especially important if the parent is taking the child out). The child's clothes are familiar and precious to them, a reminder of home and the family who provided them. To refuse to use them can hurt the child's and family's feelings and confirm the parent's worst fears about 'foster carers'.

Parents of abused children may be especially fearful that their child will transfer their affection to the carer and will want to stay with them. Parents need many reassurances from the carer, most particularly that their child's love and loyalty will remain theirs and that there is no competition for these. Parents also need to hear that they will be consulted and expected to make choices and decisions about their child, and that foster carers will maintain this practice.

Parents also need to know that relatives who are important to the child will be welcome at the foster home and the carer needs to observe interactions between the child and extended family members. It may be, for instance, that the child has a stronger attachment to the grandmother than to the mother.

The degree of contact between child and parents will have been discussed and decided upon when the contract was agreed. Although intensive access restricts both carer and parents it can, if sensitively handled by both carer and social worker, indicate the parents' commitment to the child and the child's attachment to the parents.

Parents may use some of the visiting time to talk to the carer about their own problems. It will be helpful to listen but may be wiser to say little as one's comments may be misinterpreted or repeated to the parents' legal adviser and used in evidence in court. Parents value and appreciate an honest response in language which they understand.

Records

Visits by parents and relatives to an abused child are usually supervised either by the social worker or by the carer, and observations of the family's interactions should be recorded as soon as possible after the family have left the foster home. These records may include:

– the child's feelings and behaviour before the visit

– the child's manner in welcoming one or both parents, and whether they hide and have to be coaxed to see the parent(s)

– whether the child stays in the room during the visit or finds excuses to leave and refuses to come near until one or both parents have left

– the child's demeanour, and behaviour during the visit, whether relaxed or not

– any physical contact between the parent(s) and child, and who initiated it, for instance whether the child is cuddled, and sits on either parent's lap

– whether the child plays happily with either or both parents.

The notes should conclude with the child's reaction to the parents' departure, whether they are upset, relieved, indifferent or angry. The carer's own opinion should be noted separately. Gathering this information and recording it accurately will help those concerned with the child to make the right decisions and plans for the future.

Parents have a right to know that notes will be kept about the visits, with dates, times and observations of all that occurs, and that these will be shared with the social worker. It should also be explained that these notes will either be presented or summarised at statutory reviews, and that the carer may be called to give evidence in court proceedings. Carers should assure themselves that a social worker has explained this to the parents before the child is placed.

Helping the child

The first step towards helping the child is for the carer to believe that the child is blameless. If the carer feels that the child is to blame in some way it will not be possible to respond spontaneously to the child. It is easy to become obsessed with the sexual abuse aspect, but dwelling on it as something separate from the child's overall needs can inhibit the development of a relationship between carer and child. To be nurtured the child needs spontaneous affection from both carers, for example a kiss on the cheek or an arm around the shoulder, and the carers need to feel comfortable sitting the child on their laps for a cuddle. If carers feel that they have to consider every move before it is made the abuse will become a barrier between them and the child.

The child may well need 'specialist help' towards the best possible recovery, but the carer provides a safe, caring environment which is in itself therapeutic. The carer helps children to build their self-image and self-esteem by using every opportunity to show them that they are important and of high value. Children need to hear that abuse has not damaged them for ever and that other people are unaware of it because it does not show.

Both parents and carers may participate in making a life story book by providing photographs and information to be recorded. The book will belong to the child, to go with them whether returning home or moving to a new family. Some children have to accept that they cannot return home, but when there has been honesty about decisions made, this may not come as quite such an unexpected shock. Some feelings of separation and loss may resurface again, or there may be feelings of relief. A child may regret that they disclosed abuse or even deny that the abuse took place as they fantasise about their life at home. All children need help to resolve some of these feelings while they wait for a new family. When the family has been found it is important for a child to see that the present carers like and trust them. Children need to be given the opportunity to say 'goodbye' to people of their choice, including birth parents where appropriate, and to receive permission from them to accept the new family's love and care. A special goodbye tea at the foster home and a farewell gift can make the move a positive and memorable event.

Conclusion

All fostered children deserve a high standard of care that meets their physical and emotional needs. Sexually abused children deserve recognition of the abuse and appropriate skilled help. It is the responsibility of the local authority to provide training programmes for carers in order that the necessary skills can be acquired. Equally, it is the responsibility of carers to recognise their need for training and to avail themselves of opportunities offered. Working in isolation is dangerous and mirrors the isolation of the children. If children are to survive their abuse, carers must be enabled to carry out their task. To achieve this they need help and support from other foster carers, social workers and specialists in the field of sexual abuse.

10 Managing sexually abused children in substitute families: common dilemmas in practice

Vivek Kusumakar

Dr Vivek Kusumakar is a consultant child and adolescent psychiatrist in Edinburgh. He and his team offer consultation and consultancy to social workers supervising children who are experiencing particular difficulty, and they often work alongside the social workers in seeking a resolution. In this final chapter he describes four scenarios, amalgamating cases from his practice, demonstrating formulation, treatment and the way forward. He believes that many families have strengths that are unacknowledged and that bringing these to the surface during preparatory training may well create the confidence needed to survive the vicissitudes of a difficult placement later.

Introduction

A significant number of children and adolescents who are placed in foster or adoptive families are the victims of inappropriate sexual experiences. However, sexual abuse is only one of many traumas that these young people have had to live through. The challenges that face foster and adoptive parents in the reparenting and rehabilitation of these children is enormous and cannot be overestimated. Children and adolescents who have been sexually abused exhibit not only the emotions, behaviour and relationship patterns influenced by loss, rejection and deprivation, but also the pain and confusion associated with sexual trauma.

This chapter discusses common dilemmas encountered by foster and adoptive families who have taken in children or adolescents who were sexually abused before being placed.

The seductive child; the child who masturbates excessively and in public; the child who experiments sexually with another child in the family; the child who shows sexually abusive behaviour; the child with gender-identity difficulties; the omnipotent or shut-off child who shows little need for parents; the enraged and aggressive child; the self-destructive or self-harming child; and the child with excessive bodily fears: are not uncommon examples.

However, it would be too simplistic to view these children's difficulties as emanating only from their families of origin or their sub-cultural experiences. The responses of helping agencies and professionals, and the quality of relationships, personality character- istics and stresses within the substitute families interact with the issues of the child to exacerbate difficulties or promote resilience in the child and family. Foster and adoptive parents bring their own 'baggage' into family life: emotional and behavioural responses determined by their own life experiences, early relationships and value-systems. Thus, gender, sexual, sociocultural and racial value- systems; experiences of sexual or other relationship trauma; issues around childlessness and sterility; quality of marital relationships; and degree of intra- and interpersonal turmoil in these families will significantly influence the rehabilitation of the child or adolescent who has been sexually abused in the past.

The following accounts are from practice in an interdisciplinary Child, Adolescent and Family Psychiatry (CAFP) team with a strong community-oriented service and are intended to provoke thought and debate rather than act as a 'cook-book' for practitioners.

In order to protect the identity of people involved, two or more cases have been combined to produce each vignette. Although in clinical practice many placements are disrupted, the material used in this chapter comes from families where no disruption of placement occurred and where, in fact, children and families made significant positive changes all around. Needless to say, disruption may well occur in situations similar to those described below and is often related to threshholds of tolerance and coping as well as to the degree to which children, families and helping systems are 'stuck'. One has to recognise that in some instances the disruption of a placement, rather than being a 'failure', may be the right decision for a child or family. However, it places a burden on helping agencies who are striving to stop the cycles of loss and feelings of rejection that children often experience.

The C family
Mr and Mrs C, a couple in their early thirties, had been childless for five years before they decided to adopt a child. Three years later John, aged four, was placed with them. The adoption was formalised eight months after the initial placement.

John had been sexually abused by his birth mother's boyfriend over a couple of years before it was discovered. He was taken into care on account of his mother's inability to care for him due to her alcoholism. He had no siblings. John had been with temporary foster parents for ten months before he came to the C family.

John was a clingy child and demanded to have his adoptive mother near him all the time. He had to be fed by her, bathed by her, put to bed by her and comforted by her when distressed. She found it exhausting. Attempts to get John and his adoptive father to spend more time together had not been successful, as John had become very distressed if his mother was not there as well. Mr C felt rejected by John and could barely hide his plummeting self-confidence and anger while Mrs C, feeling increasingly burdened, began to blame her husband for not trying hard enough. Their social worker, who had known them before John was placed with the family, had suggested a variety of reasonable and sensible techniques: John and his father to play together for an hour a day while his mother was in the room; the two to go out together to a local park, which John loved; John to be put to bed by Mr C, with his mother joining in; Mr C to take John to the play-group. All these attempts had been useful for brief periods, but soon John would become inconsolable unless his mother took over.

The social worker made a referral to the Child, Adolescent and Family Psychiatry Department. Rather than 'take over the case' from the social worker, who was very experienced and skilled, the CAFP team offered in the first instance to meet with her for consultation on a fortnightly basis over four sessions. It was decided that the adoptive parents could join the social worker in these sessions if she wished. It was felt that John, who appeared cheerful and relaxed if his mother was around, would not be seen at this stage by the CAFP team.

The social worker, after much discussion with Mr and Mrs C, had decided that the three of them would seek consultation together. At the first meeting, the CAFP team, consisting of a psychiatrist and an occupational therapist for this particular case, focused on the model of consultation practised by their team, which was to understand and explore the following:

– each person's concerns

– the assets and limitations of relationships with John

– the couple's relationship

– the relationship between the social worker and the family

– the parents' own life experiences, their personalities and tempera-
ments, strengths and weaknesses, fears and fantasies

– alternative hypotheses to understand the current difficulties
between John and the parents

– a variety of solutions, which might include more formal counselling
or therapy for the parents and John.

Early on in the contact the parents and social worker shared their
view of the problems with John as follows:

– John was distrustful of his father and clinging to his mother
because of his experiences of abuse within the birth family

– John needed 'expert' psychiatric help in his own right

– if things did not improve, the parents, the mother in particular,
wanted a break from John to 'think things over'.

While fully accepting that much of John's behaviour could be
understood in the light of his experiences in his family of origin, the
consultants explored life in the current adoptive family. It emerged
that John enjoyed painting with his father, who was an accomplished
amateur artist, and going swimming with his mother, who was a
keen swimmer. Soon, the couple were able to share the following
with the consultants:

– the mother's early statements to the social worker that she did not
want to adopt a handicapped or sexually abused child

– the couple's difficulties in coming to terms with the father's
sterility and his reluctance to consider adoption

– their marital difficulties, apparently triggered by Mrs C's close
relationship with her elder sister, who was perceived by Mr C as
being intrusive.

There was a dramatic response to the question 'Has anybody in your
families been hurt or abused as a child or teenager?' Mrs C burst into
tears. With considerable difficulty she shared, for the first time in her
husband's presence, that she and her sister had been repeatedly
sexually abused by their stepfather. It was hard for her to acknowledge
this, not only because of the guilt and anger surrounding the abuse,

but also because she did not want to hurt her stepfather, who she saw also as a genuinely caring man who had nursed her own mother for several years before she died.

The couple were then able to explore and work through the following issues:

- Mr C's poor self-esteem, rooted not only in his sterility but also in their poor sexual relationship, which Mrs C was not able to understand as being a result of feelings generated by her own abuse

- Mrs C's distrust of men and her reservations at leaving her husband and John together for anything but the briefest of times

- Mr C feeling pressured into adoption and his wife feeling that, although she did not want a sexually abused child, she *had* to take on John, because if she said 'No', she would not have been offered another child. The social worker wondered aloud if her inability to address some of these issues with the couple was because of her multiple roles: finding a family for John; supporting the parents; and keeping the placement going.

During the course of this work, the parents and workers were able to see that John's difficulties, although arising primarily from his own traumatic past, were also being significantly influenced by the parents' own experiences and the effects of these on their thoughts, feelings and relationships, particularly on their threshhold of tolerance of John's distress. The parents and social worker decided to meet on their own to work on these issues at length and in depth. It was agreed that they should not try anything new with John till they felt more confident and less exhausted. This was not only to reduce performance anxiety for the parents but also to avoid premature attempts that might fail and further erode self-confidence. It was also agreed that if things got more trying and exhausting, it would be good for John and his parents to have a break from one another, with John spending a long weekend with the family of an aunt who was willing to help.

Within eight weeks of weekly sessions with their social worker, Mr and Mrs C announced that they wanted to try again some of the things they had attempted unsuccessfully in the past: the father spending more time with John and giving the mother a break; the mother and father, together, stating clearly to John that they knew he had been hurt in the past and that 'Mummy and Daddy are not going to hurt you. We will keep you safe'; and John having regular times with his mother, swimming, or with his father, painting.

At a review meeting the parents happily said that things were much better, that John was more settled and that they linked this change to their own growing robustness. They felt less disabled and persecuted by John's distress, they trusted each other more, and were noticeably less exhausted. They seemed to be enjoying John.

The R family

Shirley, a 13-year-old, had been placed with the R family on a long-term fostering contract, after having been taken into care following extensive physical and sexual abuse by her mother and stepfather over many years. Two previous short-term foster placements had broken down within weeks because the foster families were unable to cope with her public masturbation and sexually seductive behaviour.

Although Mr and Mrs R were told about Shirley's experience of sexual and physical abuse, they had not been told about her seductive behaviour or the problem with excessive masturbation. The placement agency wanted to give Shirley a 'fresh start'.

The R family consisted of two biological children, Alice aged 24 and Andy aged 21, both of whom had full-time jobs yet continued to live in the family home. There was another foster child in the family, 16-year-old Robin. Robin had been with the family for over three years, having been placed there after being taken into care for running away from a violent, drug-addict mother and living rough on the streets.

Shirley shared a room with Alice, while Robin and Andy shared another room. After an initial quiescent period the family, particularly Mrs R and Alice, expressed their concern and disgust as Shirley masturbated for long periods in her bed and sometimes in the living room while watching TV, and behaved 'seductively' towards Mr R, Andy and Robin. Robin had become so anxious after Shirley touched his 'privates', that he had run away from home and had been returned to the family by the police, who found him begging in the streets.

The R family were very angry with the social worker when they were told about Shirley's previous seductive and masturbatory behaviour. They insisted that Shirley get psychiatric treatment, hence the referral to the CAFP team.

The CAFP team, consisting of a psychologist and psychiatrist, met for the first time in the family home with the whole family and the social worker. The purpose of this meeting was to explore the functioning of the foster family, listen to people's concerns and assess the family's ability to stick with Shirley. The meeting was held in the evening with the express purpose of including Alice and Andy in sessions, as they appeared to be affected by or at least knew about Shirley's behaviour. At the first meeting it became clear that Mr and Mrs R had sought referral to 'external experts' because of their anger and distrust of the social worker as he had not shared Shirley's previous behaviour with them.

Over a couple of family sessions the following points were acknowledged:

- Shirley's masturbation disturbed Alice and kept her awake at night

- Andy and Robin were frightened by Shirley's seductive behaviour, which consisted of Shirley touching their genitals and standing up close to them

- Mr R felt that Shirley was trying to trap him into doing things he did not want to do

- Mrs R was convinced that Shirley had become 'addicted' to sexual contact following her sexual abuse

- Shirley was preoccupied with anxious thoughts that she would be ejected from the R family, her anxiety increasing her masturbatory behaviour.

Shirley also felt very guilty and tended to show atonement behaviour by becoming very servile towards members of the family, who felt further threatened rather than reassured by this. A considerable amount of anger was expressed towards the social worker by the family and Shirley for not telling them about some of Shirley's previous problems and for not barring contact with Shirley's birth mother. The consultants decided to include the social worker as co-therapist rather than let him be isolated and 'picked off' by the family system. This was done intentionally so as to enable Shirley and the foster family to integrate the good and bad in the therapists and, in the process, come to terms with the good and bad in themselves rather than seeing all badness resting in Shirley.

In addition to whole-family sessions, the foster parents were seen by the social worker and psychologist, and the children by the psychiatrist. During these collateral sessions it emerged that Mrs R was afraid that Mr R might be seduced by Shirley, as he had had an affair with an 18-year-old woman only two years after their marriage. Mrs R also said that she felt angry and let down by her husband because this affair was when she was working hard looking after their first child, and now, again, he only wanted to have 'nice' contact with Shirley, excluding himself from any situation that demanded his being strict with her. When Shirley sat on his knee and 'touched herself', Mrs R was upset that, rather than being firm in stopping her, Mr R had done nothing at the time but later on had joked about it with his wife. Much of the work with the couple centred around helping them examine issues of trust in their relationship. At the same time they were counselled about the need for clear, concrete messages to limit Shirley's sexually inappropriate behaviour while ensuring that they did not reject her. They were encouraged to say to Shirley things like: 'It is okay to sit next to me, but it is not okay to touch my privates', 'You can touch yourself if you want to, but do it in private, not when any of us is around', 'When you grow up and make friends with somebody you like and who likes you, it is okay to touch, kiss or have sex, but it is not okay to do this with your brothers, sisters or parents', and so on. Mr R was helped to also acknowledge that Shirley's behaviour, although inappropriate, was titillating. Further, the couple were channelled towards exploring why their grown-up children, although living at home, did not contribute towards expenses. Mr R said that this had been a serious bone of contention between himself and his wife: he had wanted her to 'let go'and insist that Alice and Andy become more independent. She, on the other hand, felt that the world was cruel and harsh and that they should stay at home for as long as possible. Mr R then accused his wife of putting a 'chastity belt' on the children. He thought it was unusual, if not abnormal, not to have friends of the opposite sex at their age. Mrs R, who had had a puritanical, religious upbringing, saw sex as 'bad and dirty'. Considerable work had to be done with the couple about these value-systems and beliefs, which had been so strongly challenged by Shirley's behaviour.

In the sessions with the young people the following areas were covered:

- Robin's childhood deprivation and rejection by his mother, and how this resembled Shirley's life

- Shirley's difficulties in being angry with her birth mother, with the result that she displaced her anger onto others and still carried a heavy burden of guilt for what had happened to her

- masturbation, although developmentally normal, was excessive in this situation, probably as a result of anxiety about the future and a need for comfort

- Shirley's seductive behaviour was an attempt to prove that people liked her and that she could control people

- Alice and Andy's ambivalence about masturbation and other sexually exciting activity and their fears that they would get into messy relationships with one another if sex played a part in it

- acknowledgement of each one's assets (Alice: kind, good pianist; Andy: clever, good at fixing things; Robin: good listener, good on the skateboard; Shirley: helpful, good at schoolwork; Mrs R: supportive, good cook; Mr R: humorous, good gardener)

- empathy not only for Shirley but also for the restricted life that Alice and Andy had been leading.

The parental and child subsystems were asked to feed back to each other and make healthy demands for support, help and understanding from each other. The situation had changed from the original focus of Shirley's problems to the multiple foci of the needs of the different people in the family. The family, after clear hints from Shirley, requested the social work department to restrict Shirley's meetings with her birth mother to closely supervised brief periods rather than unsupervised overnight stays. Shirley felt 'claimed' by the family and in her new-found feelings of relative security she was able to take on board the boundaries and limits that the R family provided for her. She was freed to talk more openly, albeit with considerable sadness, anger and guilt about her abuse and her relationship with her mother and step-father. The workers and family, after six months of work, supported Shirley's entry into a group for sexually abused teenagers.

Her excessive masturbation and seductiveness disappeared within the first 12 weeks of contact. During the course of treatment she showed outbursts of anger and omnipotence, but at the end of 14 months she was in group-psychotherapy, and appeared more settled although she was an adventurous and often impulsive teenager. Meanwhile, Alice and Andy left home to independent 'digs' with friends.

The A family

Edward, a 13-year-old boy, had been placed on a long-term fostering basis with Mr and Mrs A, aged 59 and 54 respectively. This came about after Edward was deemed to be out of his birth mother's control, having run away frequently and truanted from school. Further, Edward was cross-dressing and stating emphatically that he wished to have a sex-change operation. He would become miserable or extremely angry when his birth mother expressed any views about his gender identity difficulties. The history was that Edward had been chronically abused by his mother's ex-cohabitee between the ages of eight and 12 years.

The A family had two adult sons, who were married and living independently. They had regular but infrequent contact with Mr and Mrs A.

Mr and Mrs A saw Edward's desire to dress as a female and want a sex-change operation as wrong and as a sickness. They felt that, apart from giving him a safe home base with a structure and clear limits, they had to help him be a male. They did this by stopping any opportunity for him cross-dressing by keeping any female attire under lock and key, preventing him from talking about wanting to be a girl and telling him in no uncertain terms that his wish to be a girl was wrong. The family's attitude and values concerning Edward's gender identity difficulties were in contrast to the social worker's, a 38-year-old woman. She not only felt that the difficulties were a direct result of sexual abuse but also that Edward had a right to be a woman if he chose to be, and that it was wrong to suppress his desire. There had been much discussion, debate and heated argument between the social worker and the foster family. As the disagreements between them had become more obvious, so had Edward's turmoil and misery. A referral was sought to the CAFP team, in this instance consisting of a psychologist and a social worker.

The consultants from the team met initially with Mr and Mrs A and the social worker. Over two sessions details of Edward's history as well as the dilemmas in current management were discussed fully. It emerged that it was the social worker who had initiated the referral to the team. Mr and Mrs A were wary, feeling that professionals were ganging up against them and, as Mrs A put it, they were joining in these meetings because they felt they had to co-operate with the social work department. She made it clear that she was tired of people who kept saying that Edward should be allowed to continue cross-dressing. Mr and Mrs A perceived any step that was not aimed at stopping Edward from cross-dressing as encouraging him to continue. The consultants, Mr and Mrs A, and the social worker agreed that it was important to try and understand Edward's turmoil and his expressed wishes to be a girl rather than a boy.

A single joint meeting was then arranged with Edward present. Edward was told that the adults were trying to work out the best possible ways to help him and that this could only be done by understanding what he had gone through, and his thoughts and feelings about the past, present and future.

The group of adults reached a consensus that, at this stage, Mr and Mrs A should continue to do what they thought best but also that one of the consultants would meet with Edward over a few sessions while the other consultant would meet with Mr and Mrs A and the social worker.

Edward was seen over six weekly sessions, each lasting an hour. The stance of the consultant during these sessions was one of a listener seeking clarification from time to time rather than of an interrogator encouraging disclosures. The consultant acknowledged that she was aware that Edward had been sexually interfered with, had been unhappy at home, and that he had difficulties attending school as well as expressing a strong desire, through words and action, to be a girl rather than a boy. 'We can talk about some or all of these things in your own time and when you feel strong enough. It's okay for you not to share things with me unless you feel ready to. The adults who are trying to help you just now are feeling a bit stuck and need your help in trying to understand things better.' Edward had been able to say that he felt 'pissed off' and 'got at' by adults. The consultant spent a considerable time acknowledging Edward's helplessness in the face of adults doing things to him, with him and for him. His consequent feelings of frustration, anger and confrontation were explored and acknowledged. Only after this was done were any links made between his feelings at the current time and the time when he was being sexually abused. After some initial hesitancy, Edward was able to share the fact that his abuser had forced him to wear his mother's clothes while various sexual acts took place between them. Although his mother had believed him and reported her cohabitee to the police, she had told Edward that she thought he was a 'poofter'. She had also said to him that he had always been a 'sissy' and 'girlish'. He had looked at himself in the mirror on more than one occasion and felt that because he was not as strong as other boys and had blonde curly hair, his mother was right: he was meant to be a girl. Later, quite suddenly, he said that he wanted an operation to take off his penis because he would rather be a woman than a man who did nasty things to children.

Collaterally the other consultant, meeting with Mr and Mrs A and the social worker, had helped them to understand that sexual trauma in the face of emerging adolescent sexuality might explain some of Edward's difficulties. Mr and Mrs A were able to admit that they had had a very rigid and religious upbringing and saw many sexual activities as being 'deviant'. They were very blunt in their questioning of their social worker who, they felt, was sympathetic to Edward's needs to be a girl because she was a lesbian. They were surprised to hear that, although she had liberal views about people's sexual preferences, she had been married, was now divorced and had three children. Once anger and mutual distrust had been worked through, Mrs A was able to say that she was afraid that Edward might seduce her husband into a sexual contact. Mr A, in turn, could say that he had never fully agreed with his wife's views about cross-dressing, but had gone along with it because he didn't want to undermine her as 'she is the foster parent and I have another job'. At a feedback meeting, Edward was helped to share the things he had said in his individual sessions and, very soon, Mr and Mrs A viewed Edward more sympathetically.

Apart from a new, co-operative partnership between Mr and Mrs A and their social worker, the adults reached a consensus regarding the following:

– rather than provoking Edward's oppositional and helpless behaviour altogether by forbidding any cross-dressing or talk of sex change,

Edward would have time every evening for half an hour after tea to talk about whatever he wished

- he would be advised to restrict his cross-dressing to his own room
- whenever he showed age-appropriate behaviour he would be praised for it as well as given time with Mr A, repairing cars (which Mr A did as a hobby and Edward had a great interest in)
- he was persuaded to go into group psychotherapy with other teenagers
- the social worker would see the whole family together once every six weeks to discuss family life in general and how Edward and the family were coping with adolescence.

On follow-up, Edward appeared settled in terms of his peer relationships, having used his group to deal with peer issues as well as issues to do with sexual abuse and feelings of rejection. His cross-dressing continued, sporadically, in the privacy of his own room but he was able to say that he had acquired a girlfriend and had serious doubts regarding a change of sex. Edward shared with his foster parents his upset feelings about his cross-dressing and said that he wanted help to stop it altogether. He also expressed concern that he was afraid that his body was damaged or that he had AIDS. Some of these anxieties were dealt with through a physical examination and counselling regarding AIDS. Our most recent information about Edward is that he is in therapy to deal with his cross-dressing, using a combination of psychotherapy and behavioural techniques, but that some issues around this remain unresolved.

The M family

Kelly, an eight-year-old girl, had been adopted into the M family when she was six. Kelly had been ritually abused by her parents and others before she and her brother Keith, aged five, had been taken into care. Mr and Mrs M, a security guard and a policewoman respectively, had sought help from their social worker because 'Kelly does not listen to us; we cannot get through to her . . .' The social worker had worked with them for three months before becoming increasingly concerned herself with Mr and Mrs M, whom she found very negative towards Kelly. Mr and Mrs M's main complaint was that Kelly did not share any of her past with them, kept smiling all the time, and spent a lot of time at home in her room playing on her own. They also felt that she seemed to have more fun with neighbours than with them. There were no problems of discipline. The social worker, with the agreement of Mr and Mrs M, asked for consultation from the CAFP team when the parents hinted at wanting to give up Kelly. The consultant, this time a psychiatrist, agreed to join the social worker in her sessions with the parents.

At the first session Mr and Mrs M, who knew about Kelly's victimisation in her birth family, said that they had jumped at the offer of having Kelly because they felt they could help a sexually abused child. They had read a lot about sexual abuse and were particularly aware of many written accounts of in-depth psychotherapy with such children. They had done this reading as a 'preparation' before Kelly came into the family. They now felt that she was a 'closed book', 'damaged beyond repair' and that 'she would be better off in a psychiatric unit than in a family'. The social worker and psychiatrist got agreement from the parents that there would be one family session with Kelly present, two sessions with the couple, and two sessions with Kelly, as a sort of re-assessment, before an opinion could be given.

In the family session the consultant noted that Kelly was co-operative and cheerful, joining in the conversation spontaneously whenever discussing current family life. However, whenever the parents began talking about her birth family (and they attempted to do this often), she would wear a fixed smile and shield herself from questions or comments by saying 'I don't know' or by playing by herself. The parents, also, did not respond warmly to her cues to join her in play, but were open in their criticisms of her defensive behaviour when they initiated conversation about her traumatic past. Comments like 'We know you have been abused'; 'Why can't you trust mummy and daddy and tell them what happened?', and 'If we have to help you, you will have to talk to us' were in plenty in the family session.

In the individual sessions with Kelly in a playroom the consultant observed that her play was full of symbolism of aggression, destruction and atonement, and she was wary and defensive about discussing her play. She became chatty and open when talking about her life in the

M family and felt she was making them sad and angry because 'I am bad'. When she was asked about her brother, she became animated and wondered where he was. A social worker had told her he was with another family but she thought 'he is still with my real dad and mum'. She also shared worries about her adoptive mother's health, saying 'I visited mummy in hospital, but I don't know why she was there.' No interpretations were attempted in the two play sessions with her.

In the two sessions with Mr and Mrs M the discussion centred on their decision to adopt, their expectations, life before Kelly, their families of origin, and their hopes and fears for the future. Particular use was made of drawing a family and friends' tree to get an account of relationships, past and present. The highlights of these sessions were:

- there was no specific reason for their childlessness

- they wanted to adopt an abused child because they felt they could help 'repair' damage

- they were convinced that a child could be helped only after it had 'shared everything'

- since the adoption, Mrs M had developed cervical cancer, and although she had been told that the prognosis was good in her case, she was worried that she might die and, hence, felt 'I have to do all I can for Kelly and do it fast'

- their past and current family life and religious views had convinced them that a 'confessional' approach was the best one

- they harboured guilt that they had not adopted Kelly's brother, who had severe cystic fibrosis and a reduced life expectancy, although they had been told that he had been fostered by another family and had since died

- they said that they found Kelly 'shut off' and unrewarding, making them feel useless as parents

- they also felt guilt for feeling negatively towards Kelly.

Kelly was helped to share with her adoptive parents her questions about her brother and her worries about her mother's health. Helping her with these things was not only mutually rewarding for parents and child but also distracted the parents from their preoccupation with getting a disclosure from Kelly. Every effort was made to boost Mr and Mrs M's role as helpful parents by pointing out the various ways in which they were helping Kelly in the here and now.

Kelly's 'shut off' behaviour was re-labelled as her way of protecting herself from the pain of the past and her wish to make a good life in the present family. The parents were counselled on the need to respect Kelly's defences regarding past trauma and to accept her need to enact her thoughts and feelings in non-verbal play rather than words. This persuaded the parents to permit Kelly to enter individual play therapy with a child psychotherapist. Mr and Mrs M continued to work with their social worker on many of these issues, including anxieties around Mrs M's health and, on follow-up, the family appeared to have made a contented readjustment.

Conclusion

Although a multiplicity of issues have been addressed above, there is no doubt that workers face other dilemmas which have not been dealt with in this paper.

In our selection processes, prospective foster and adoptive families often feel a need to present a picture of being problem-free. Families feel that if they share a history of being abused themselves, struggling to come to terms with sterility and childlessness, having difficulties in the sexual sphere, having had extra-marital relationships and other stresses from the past and present, they might well be excluded from consideration by agencies. Clinical practice and sociological studies indicate that many of these traumatic experiences and stresses are not uncommon in ordinary families. For some families it will be true that they are severely 'disabled' by traumas; in other families, similar trauma may increase their resilience and strength. Many families may well be able to work through trauma and stress if provided with adequate help. So the 'selection' or 'screening' of families must not only find out about trauma and stress experiences, but also ascertain how such experiences have affected relationships, value systems, sensitivities and expectations, especially in the areas of sexuality, gender and power. Workers, too, should examine the bases of their own value systems so that they can sift out their own agendas from those of the families and children they are professionally involved with.

Families will be more likely to acknowledge their danger areas if their strengths are recognised by workers. Workers may also need to help families to recognise these strengths in themselves. Otherwise, when problems arise, unexpressed feelings of self-doubt and inadequacy may make the worker's offers of help feel persecutory.

We need to recognise the demands in terms of effort and expertise that are made of substitute families and workers in the management of children and adolescents who have been sexually abused. It would be useful for such families and front-line workers to have routine back-up from a sexual abuse team offering advice and therapy. For example, a common dilemma is whether a child should be persuaded to share information about past trauma, or should be left to choose his or her own time. It is often difficult for families and workers at the 'coal face' to decide about this, and a specialist back-up team can be of help, often simply by virtue of being once removed from the situation of the child and family. Above all it is important that, in organising any extra help, families and the various agencies should work together to ensure that no one is left feeling useless. Such feelings in any of the people involved can sabotage good management.